By
WILLIAM H. CONSIDINE
with
RON KIRKSEY

Copyright © 2019 by Children's Hospital Medical Center of Akron

ISBN: 978-0-9980207-3-0

Library of Congress Control Number: 2019939862

All Rights Reserved. No part of this book may be reproduced or transmitted in any form or by any means, electronic or mechanical, including photocopying, recording, or by any information storage and retrieval system without written permission from the author, except for the inclusion of brief quotations in a review.

Printed in the United States of America.

Dedication

This book on success is dedicated to my mom and dad.

Dad passed away on April 22, 2014. As of this writing, my mom is still inspiring all of us with her wit and stories. Mom and Dad had a direct role in the success I was able to realize and share with others.

I mention my parents in the chapter in this book on commitment because of the standard they set for everyone. I easily could have written about the life lessons they taught in every chapter. They lived the success formula daily, and I love them.

Thanks, Mom and Dad.

Gene and Howard Considine. Courtesy of Considine Family.

Contents

Preface vii

Introduction 1

Chapter 1: Character 5

Chapter 2: Culture 12

Chapter 3: Civility 19

Chapter 4: Caring 26

Chapter 5: Community 34

Chapter 6: Collaboration 50

Chapter 7: Communication 62

Chapter 8: Commitment 69

Chapter 9: Confidence 77

Chapter 10: Courage 84

Chapter 11: Coaching 91

Chapter 12: Corporate Citizenship 98

    Marks Family Corporate Citizenship Blue Line 100

    GAR Foundation 102

    Goodyear Tire & Rubber Company 104

    Ohio Edison/FirstEnergy Corporation 106

    Akron Paint & Varnish 109

    LeafFilter Gutter Protection 110
    Ken Babby, Akron RubberDucks 112
    Theken Family of Companies & NextStep Companies 114
    Timken Foundation 115
Afterword: Children 117
Acknowledgments 123
About the Author 125
References 129
Index 131

Preface

How do you define success, and how is it measured?

- Is success winning or losing?
- Is success monetary?
- Is success receiving a grade or a degree?
- Is success avoidance of failure?
- Is there a difference between individual and team success?
- What are the key ingredients required to achieve success?

This book discusses the elements of success as they apply to leadership. What should leaders focus on as they strive to serve others and be successful in advancing the mission of the organizations they serve? How best can a team's success empower individuals and a larger community?

As I thought about these questions and other opportunities that come with leadership, I reflected on my 50-year career in hospital administration. Forty years of that career were spent as the CEO of Akron Children's Hospital, a world-class health care and research organization.

The hospital is one of the nation's largest and oldest freestanding children's health care providers in the country, having been part of the Akron community for nearly 130 years. Akron Children's is well-known for its quality programs and culture of respect and trustworthiness. That culture dates back to 1890, and the hospital's original values remain unchanged today.

In 1890, two groups of church women routinely met and discussed the concept of service above self. Their discussions led them to look for solutions to help parents in Akron, the "Rubber City," who took their children to work with them in the downtown factories. Often, both parents worked, and no child care was available.

This was obviously a problem, interfering with production and more importantly placing children in harm's way. The air quality, temperature and noise, along with safety hazards, were threats to the children's physical and mental health.

When the two groups of women discovered they shared the same concerns, they decided to collaborate on a solution. They developed a plan to create a downtown nursery for children and proceeded to make it a reality. This effort was volunteer-driven, child- and family-focused, and based on an urgent community need.

Task one was to find a location and facility for the nursery. It just so happened that a large home owned by Colonel George Tod Perkins, whose family was among the early settlers in Akron, was vacant in the area near the factories. Col. Perkins had built another home, and his downtown property was available.

The women approached Col. Perkins with their idea for a nursery and asked if they could use the main floor of the home. He liked the idea and answered "Yes." To honor his generosity, the women decided to name the nursery after his granddaughter, so it became the Mary Day Nursery.

The next task was to develop a child- and family-focused daily schedule. The volunteers arranged the first floor of the house according to the ages of the children and developed activities that included reading, math, art, music, play time, nap time and more.

This concept was kindergarten before its time. In fact, it was noticed by Akron school officials and subsequently replicated in the city's schools as official kindergarten.

The volunteers set a price of 5 cents for a half day and 10 cents for a full day. But they let everyone know if families couldn't afford the fee, their children were still welcome. The women held linen and bake sales and other events to raise operating funds for the nursery. When they were ready to officially open, they decided to

SuCCess

Mary Day Nursery in 1896. Courtesy of Akron Children's Hospital.

place three promises on the wall behind the reception desk to greet everyone who entered the home.

- Promise One: We promise to treat every child who enters these doors as if that child is our own.
- Promise Two: We promise to treat you the way you want to be treated.
- Promise Three: We promise never to turn a child away for any reason.

WOW! The Mary Day Nursery opened and became the pride of the community. It was based on values, volunteering and helping children. All expectations were exceeded, and the positive energy was palpable.

One day, an ill child who needed medical attention was brought to the nursery. The volunteers knew the promises and wanted to treat this child as they would their own. They talked with the parents and together reached out to a physician who came to the nursery, treated the child and followed the young lad to recovery.

Word of that kindness from the nursery spread through the factories. Overnight, the Mary Day Nursery was overwhelmed with children who needed medical care.

The volunteers again saw a need and wanted to respond through their service-above-self passion. The group again approached Col. Perkins and shared with him the idea of converting the second floor of the house into an infirmary for children. Col. Perkins recognized the need, agreed with the idea and donated the entire house to the volunteers so they could advance their new program.

The second floor had a very large room that was transformed into a ward for children. Beds and cots were placed along the walls. Other rooms on the floor became treatment and even operating rooms. The medical community responded favorably, as did corporate leaders and the general public. In this way, Akron

Children on the front porch of the Mary Day Nursery, 1917. Courtesy of Akron Children's Hospital.

SUCCESS

Children's Hospital was born, based on a foundation of volunteerism and promises.

From that humble beginning, Akron Children's has grown into one of the nation's largest freestanding, independent, community-governed children's hospitals.

The keys to the success of those early volunteers were that they were caring, collaborative, courageous, committed, community-focused, good communicators and confident; they also embraced citizenship and civility and were people of character who created a culture that is still thriving. They were admired champions for children.

The Akron Children's organization today consists of two hospital campuses in Akron and Boardman, a growing number of regional health centers, 30 pediatrician offices, numerous specialty care services located throughout the region, a home care service

Aerial photo of Akron Children's Hospital campus, late 1960s. Courtesy of Akron Children's Hospital.

and a school nurse program serving more than 30 local school districts. It also includes a population health company, a neonatal network currently in six adult hospitals, inpatient pediatric units or providers in three partner hospitals, an active foundation and numerous affiliations in the many communities served by the hospital throughout Ohio and western Pennsylvania.

In 2018, we had the privilege of providing more than 1.1 million patient visits through our inpatient and outpatient programs.

The promises placed on the wall of the nursery in 1890 are still alive, and they are the foundation of today's still-evolving Akron Children's Hospital.

We know the future is bright, despite any challenges we may face, because this community believes in its children.

That's our success story. What's yours?

Aerial photo of Akron Children's Hospital campus today. Courtesy of Akron Children's Hospital.

Introduction

'VE ALWAYS BEEN PARTIAL to the letter C. It's tied to my last name, Considine, and reflects the grades I usually received from the nuns at St. Mary Crusaders Elementary School.

I dated my wife, Becky, when she lived on Chitty Avenue, and we named our daughter Cathryn Christine. I also read along the way that C students make excellent CEOs because of their street smarts, instincts, social skills and more. I'm sticking with that story.

Children is another great word that starts with the letter C, which led to my thoughts on how to define success. These priorities have influenced my work over the past 50 years. They have informed my value system and enriched my life's journey.

This book discusses in more detail how important character, culture, civility and caring are to success, as well as community, collaboration, communication, commitment, confidence, courage, coaching and corporate citizenship.

What additional words starting with C come to mind when you try to define success in your life and the lives of others?

I have written 12 chapters that share my thoughts on success, and each explores a word beginning with the letter C. These chapters feature people who have influenced my life and possess the skill identified. I hope these individuals and their stories will remind you of others whose character traits help define success in business and life.

The chapters describe words beginning with the letter C that, from my experience, influence leadership and success. These include catalyst, creative, constructive, courteous, charisma, conscientious, compassion, charming, considerate, change, calm and collegial. They are some of the many traits that might comprise a person's leadership style and their formula for success. There are numerous other traits beginning with C that may have more meaning to you, the reader.

Think about what type of formula would work for you to bring out the best in the teams and organizations you represent.

In writing this book, my intent is to inspire you to reflect on your own successes and leadership aspirations. I also want to share the lessons on success I have learned from the people who influenced my life.

The champions in this book are men and women I have known as a child and student, or colleagues I've worked with over the years. All these individuals affirmed the early lessons passed on to me by my parents.

My personal success as a leader, mentor and lifelong learner is reflected in the way I embraced civility, courage in decision-making, collaboration, transparent communication and enabled a caring, just culture; promoted our community and fostered corporate citizenship throughout the organization I led; coached and mentored future leaders by modeling the best behavior; and advocated for the health and well-being of all children.

These qualities defined my 40-year tenure as the CEO of a children's hospital. My character and career were shaped by the inspiration, strength and courage of the children served by Akron Children's Hospital and the lessons I learned from the successful people I met along the way.

In these pages you will find advice on achieving career success, but this is far from the only definition of a successful life. Bill Sheridan, who writes for the Business Learning Institute blog, summed up the closing keynote speech given at an accounting and technology conference by retired BKD CEO Neal Spencer. In his remarks, Spencer cited the following passage from Ralph Waldo Emerson's poem "Success" to illustrate the difference between thriving and merely surviving:

Success

What is success? To laugh often and much; to win the respect of intelligent people and the affection of children; to earn the appreciation of honest critics and endure the betrayal of false friends; to appreciate beauty; to find the best in others; to leave the world a bit better, whether by a healthy child, a garden patch or a redeemed social condition; to know even one life has breathed easier because you have lived. This is to have succeeded.

This book ends with an afterword on children who also seemed to have been on Emerson's mind. In this final section, I share my thoughts on the challenges facing children today and how it is our responsibility to invest in their future success. The time is now for us to place a priority on all children—to promote their right to health, education, safety and equal opportunity.

The chapters in this book speak to the values embedded in my DNA. Each person will have their own success formula. After reading this book, I encourage you to reflect on your own plan for success and share it with others through your actions and behavior.

I hope and trust you will enjoy success—both reading about it in this book and achieving it in your life!

Chapter 1
Character

IT'S A LONG WAY from loading trucks for $2 an hour to owning the company, expanding it into numerous other properties and building your own charitable foundation along the way. Philip H. Maynard has lived that journey, and he still seems humbled by his life experiences.

"That boss saw something in me that I didn't see in myself," Phil said of his early job at the warehouse. Undoubtedly, what that first boss saw was Maynard's character.

When Phil returned to Akron after his military service during the Vietnam War, he enrolled at The University of Akron to complete his college education. That's when he went to work at the warehouse loading dock.

The owner soon discovered the character and talent Phil brought to the company. His ability to inspire co-workers, lead them to work as a team and gain credibility through his own work ethic really had an impact on the warehousing and storage operations. He received a variety of promotions and eventually was in a position to take ownership of the company. That company, Akron Storage and Warehouse, grew under his leadership.

Now his workday begins in a welcoming, wood-paneled office in the headquarters of the Maynard Family Foundation, housed in a building still surrounded by warehouses, truck traffic and his business, ASW Properties, Ltd.

"Character is when you can look in the mirror and see that you've done your best," Phil said. "It's being ethical, moral, never hurting anyone and having respect for your fellow man."

Phil lives those values through his foundation by providing funds where the money will do the most good—not necessarily by funding the flashiest projects. "I invest in people, not businesses," he said.

Phil Maynard is the perfect representative for this chapter on character.

There is a program known as Character Counts!® that was developed by the Joseph and Edna Josephson Institute of Ethics. The program was brought to my attention when I was chairing an Akron task force looking into youth violence. Leaders of our public schools were interested in incorporating the Character Counts! message into the daily curriculum. At Akron Children's, we were very impressed with the message and decided to build these character components into our employees' annual evaluations.

The Character Counts! program promotes six pillars of character: trustworthiness, respect, responsibility, fairness, caring and citizenship. These pillars are on a script in my mind, and I continually reflect on them in everything I do. In addition, during my annual evaluation with the hospital board's Governance Committee, we discuss how I demonstrate these traits and identify areas for potential improvement. The process has benefited the entire organization.

Leadership textbooks discuss the importance of character. Women and men of character have truly influenced me to believe in their vision.

For instance, trustworthiness has been a key element of the hospital's philosophy of family-centered health care. Who would want to leave their child with an organization or people they don't trust? Trust comes from actions, transparency, truthfulness, experience, quality and inclusiveness.

Character traits, both good and bad, have been the subject of evaluations, writings and research. Leadership is influenced by an individual's character. Success is also influenced by an individual's character.

So, what is character? And how do we define character as it relates to successful leadership?

Merriam-Webster states that character applies to "the aggregate of moral qualities by which a person is judged apart from intelligence, competence or special talents," and it defines character as "one of the attributes or features that make up and distinguish an individual." Character can also be referred to as personality, disposition, temperament and nature.

In short, the character of an individual is a key ingredient in developing trusting relationships. A person of character is viewed as being truthful and credible. People defer to individuals with high moral character because they trust these individuals to do what's right.

I've always responded positively to men and women of character. Their actions speak for themselves. They are sensitive to others, know their audience and are genuine. I've found people of character to be respectful, trustworthy, caring, responsible, inclusive, positive and honest. Individuals of character unite, empower and excite people, and become popular and admired leaders. Their leadership and the moral qualities that comprise their character lead to their success.

This brings us back to Phil Maynard, a great example of a person of character. Phil is a local Akron-area guy, born to a modest, hardworking family. His parents instilled in him a sound value and belief system. He developed a strong work ethic and attitude of service to others. His character development was grounded in faith, family and honesty. These elements were supported by his humility and hunger for learning.

Phil attended Archbishop Hoban High School in Akron and was involved in community service projects as well as academic pursuits. Following high school, he enrolled at Kent State University. During the Vietnam conflict, Phil enlisted in the U.S. Army Intelligence Agency and was stationed in the Far East. While there he met his wife, Tomiko. They've been married for 50 years, and have two married daughters and six grandchildren.

While Phil and Tomiko were raising their family, he was devoting countless hours to ASW. He was also involved in community and professional organizations. He was the go-to person for entrepreneurs and a variety of not-for-profit organizations. His generosity with his time, talent and treasure enriched numerous organizations and people. He's been a mentor to a who's who of men and women throughout the country. The moral qualities that are the foundation of his character serve as standards to all his associates, friends and acquaintances.

"Your idea of success changes over the years," Phil told me. "When you're young, you're interested in financial security, meeting the right people and, I suppose, adding to your prestige.

"But as you get older, success is more about accomplishments, successfully completing a project and making something better. Success is really about leaving a better world," he said.

Early in my friendship with Phil, I asked if he could arrange a meeting with his then-boss, the owner of the company. My objective was to ask his boss to consider making a generous donation to a project at Akron Children's Hospital. Phil agreed to help set up the meeting but said he would leave the philanthropic ask to me.

I remember the early morning meeting very well. Phil's boss was welcoming when we met in his office. When I shared my appreciation for the meeting and let him know I wanted him to consider a gift to the hospital, he became very serious and inquisitive. We discussed in detail the proposed project, which would benefit our patients and families, as well as the needed funds.

Phil sat in the room and quietly watched the interaction between his boss and me. His boss was a shrewd businessman and a well-known negotiator.

Following a one-hour discussion, I thanked Phil's boss for meeting with me, said I appreciated his consideration of the request and asked him to let me know if he needed additional information.

Success

The owner acknowledged that we were both plenty busy and didn't need more meetings. He said he would support the project with a $150,000 gift: he would contribute $75,000 and Phil would do the same!

This was news to Phil, and with his salary at the time, it was a challenge. We ended the meeting and departed. Phil laughed at what occurred and was pleased the hospital would receive a gift. He also assured me he would figure out how to hold up his end of the deal, and he did. He was a person of character throughout the entire process.

Phil has shared his talents with many organizations. Here's a list of some of them:

- Akron-Canton Regional Foodbank
- Akron Children's Hospital
- Akron Community Foundation
- Akron Rotary Camp
- Archbishop Hoban High School
- Battered Women's Shelter
- Catholic Charities
- Heart to Heart Communications
- Leadership Akron
- OPEN M Ministries
- United Way

The greater Akron community has honored Phil and his exemplary character with several awards, two of which deserve special mention.

The first is the H. Peter Burg Award, presented annually by the Greater Akron Chamber of Commerce. The award honors the late Peter Burg, former CEO of FirstEnergy Corp. and also a man of enormous character. Pete loved his community, brought people together and, like Phil, came from humble beginnings. Pete and Phil shared a belief in people, and people believed in them because of the quality of their characters.

The second award is the Bert A. Polsky Humanitarian Award, presented annually by the Akron Community Foundation. Phil Maynard was a unanimous selection because of who he is. He's always reaching out to others, bringing people together, sharing his stories and being there for everyone. His humanitarian spirit is inspiring and has enriched our entire community.

Nineteenth-century American writer Albert Pike could have been talking about Phil when he said, "What we have done for ourselves alone dies with us; what we have done for others and the world remains and is immortal."

Phil's most recent challenge came a few years ago when he was diagnosed with a rare and aggressive cancerous tumor. He researched his options and maintained a positive, can-do attitude throughout the process. He continued to embrace his busy schedule, showed concern for others and met his responsibilities. Once he decided on a course of action, he endured aggressive interventions including surgery, proton therapy and more.

Phil's character was on display in highly visible ways. He set a standard of behavior that inspired all the members of his medical team, fellow patients, family and friends. All the elements of this man's value system proved how much character counts.

Phil said his battle with cancer had a revealing side effect. While he was undergoing the difficult treatment in Texas, his daughter set up a CaringBridge account for him. This not-for-profit social media platform hosts websites for people experiencing a health crisis that provide an easy way for supporters to check on their progress and leave notes of encouragement.

Phil's account received more than 12,500 hits during the short time it was active online. Many messages, he said, were friends checking in on him daily. But numerous others left notes of thanks for small favors, grants or other aid Phil had given them over the years.

"They would say, 'You helped us make Christmas one year,' or 'We were able to replace our windows one winter, thanks to your

SuCCess

Phil and Tomiko Maynard with their children and grandchildren. Courtesy of Maynard Family.

help,' or 'Your grant got me through college,'" Phil said. "Just little things, but you never know what will make a difference in someone's life.

"I tell my grandchildren to make an impact," Phil said. "We can all make an impact."

People of character understand the responsibilities of leadership and know the formula for creating and sustaining success.

Keys to Character

- Be respectful
- Accept responsibility
- Be trustworthy
- Be caring
- Be an engaged citizen
- Be truthful and credible
- Have a positive outlook
- Be honest and fair
- Unite and empower people

Chapter 2
Culture

WE'VE ALL HEARD THE statement, "Culture beats strategy daily."
An organization's culture is an important part of its branding, and an organization's brand goes far beyond its name, logo or website. It's very much the presence felt by visitors, employees and clients.

I witnessed that presence when I joined Akron Children's Hospital. Akron Children's possesses a strong, recognizable culture that is ingrained in the organization through its history, dedication to mission and, especially, the people who work there.

Culture is the lifeblood of any organization and an essential element to sustainable success. You sense an organization's culture when you enter its doors or interact with its people. A rich organizational culture depends on a well-understood and meaningful mission. The entire workforce believes in that mission, exemplifies its values and expresses its importance.

If an organization's workforce cannot define the mission, there is a serious, even fatal, disconnect within the organization.

The culture of an organization must be based on sound beliefs and values. The history and traditions of the organization offer stories that the workforce hears and proudly shares with others. The culture of an organization also invests in those workers and values them as individuals. This is accomplished through opportunities for continuous learning, wellness programs, empowering people,

SuCCess

ongoing communications and constantly promoting a respectful, honest and genuine atmosphere.

The focus on sound beliefs and values promotes a culture that respects the past and encourages innovation and creativity for a bright future. People are re-energized daily in this type of culture. It's important to note that actions speak louder than words in maintaining a positive culture.

Words alone fool no one. They have to be matched with positive actions and a nurturing environment.

The Akron Children's Hospital I joined as CEO in 1979 was known for its family-centered care culture. The champion of that culture was Roger Sherman, who served as the CEO of Akron Children's for 36 years before his retirement.

At that time, Akron Children's had just over 1,200 employees, and they believed that Mr. Sherman knew all of them by

Roger Sherman with a patient. Courtesy of Akron Children's Hospital.

their first name. He managed by walking around and was always approachable.

The hospital grew substantially in size to address the two polio epidemics in the 1940s and 1950s. The staff, community and entire Akron Children's family were rallied by Mr. Sherman and responded to the enormous demand for health care.

A great example of the culture that bound the hospital and community together was evident in 1952 during a peak period in one of the polio epidemics. Anyone who lived through those times remembers what a frightening disease polio was for children, adults and families.

Akron Children's was one of the nation's largest polio centers, caring for both adults and children. The demand for care exceeded

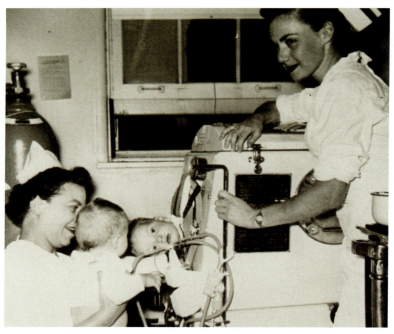

Akron Children's Hospital nurses with a polio patient in an iron lung. Courtesy of Akron Children's Hospital.

the hospital's capacity, so it approached a neighboring church. The church offered to convert its facility into a polio ward to help meet the community's needs.

At one point, as patients were being supported by iron lungs, a city-wide power outage compromised the generators supporting the patients housed in the church. Staff immediately flagged down passing motorists, who willingly stopped and assisted by manually operating the pumps powering the numerous iron lungs that provided necessary assisted breathing for the polio patients. The power outage lasted two hours, yet the culture of the hospital and supportive response of a caring community prevailed.

The community, in fact, showed it understood the hospital's culture of caring, and the crisis strengthened that culture.

Akron Children's mission of family-centered patient care, training tomorrow's caregivers through our educational programs, conducting research and serving our community was well understood by everyone. The stories of the bond between our caregivers and patient families constantly provide inspiration to Akron Children's culture.

As noted earlier, Akron Children's was founded in 1890 by a group of volunteer women who opened a nursery that was the forerunner of the hospital. The nursery was based on the three promises that are still alive today. Mr. Sherman's actions complemented the culture, and Akron Children's exuded a welcoming environment based around those core promises.

I inherited that culture in 1979. I hear routinely from visitors, families, new employees and others that they immediately get a sense of the hospital's culture when they enter our doors.

An organization projects visual cues about its culture. Our people say hello, are helpful, make eye contact, and are courteous and caring.

Our people are valued. We invest in them through programs such as tuition assistance, a leadership academy, career coaching and developmental opportunities. The culture has enabled the hospital to meet challenges and pursue opportunities to care for more children through new programs.

Obviously, your people are your culture. That culture has led to the hospital's continued growth. To operate our health care system in 2019, we employ more than 6,300 people in our workforce, have a $1 Billion operating budget and, most importantly, in 2018 we provided care at more than 1.1 million patient visits.

The hospital has come far since the beginning when a group of volunteer women established the Mary Day Nursery for children. But the underlying culture is an unbroken chain connecting the past to the present.

When our board of directors discusses our strengths and the key elements needed to fulfill our mission, our culture tops the list. A culture that is focused on service above self, on people and on trusting relationships is the foundation for all we do.

Roger Sherman built the foundation that sustains and nurtures our culture. Culture is essential for success, personal growth and satisfaction. Culture brings people together in a positive, proactive way. Effective leaders, like Mr. Sherman, understand the need to be champions and stewards of their organizations.

The hospital's *Spirit of Service* newsletter recently published a reminder about the importance of our mission and culture—one that has been used by many hospitals throughout the country and can be adapted for any organization.

You Are This Hospital

You are what people see when they arrive here.

Yours are the eyes they look into when they're frightened and lonely.

Yours are the voices people hear when they ride the elevators and

SUCCESS

when they try to sleep and when they
try to forget their problems.

You are what they hear on their way to appointments
which could affect their destinies. And what they hear
after they leave those appointments.

Yours are the comments people hear
when you think they can't.

Yours is the intelligence and caring that people hope
they'll find here.

If you're noisy, so is the hospital. If you're rude,
so is the hospital.

And if you're wonderful—so is the hospital.

No visitors, no patients can ever know the <u>real</u> you,

the you that <u>you</u> know is there—unless you let them see it.

All they can know is what they see
and hear and experience.

And so, we have a stake in your attitude
and in the collective

attitudes of everyone who works at the hospital.

We are judged by your performance.

We are the care <u>you</u> give, the attention <u>you</u> pay,
the courtesies <u>you</u> extend.

We are the culture.

WILLIAM H. CONSIDINE

What's your definition of culture? What are your examples of an inspiring culture?

> **Keys to Culture**
>
> - Understand the past
> - Respect others
> - Be responsible for your actions
> - Be honest and trustworthy
> - Keep your bad hair day to yourself

Chapter 3
Civility

ANOTHER IMPORTANT WORD THAT starts with C is civility. What is civility, and why is it important to success? How do you even define civility in today's world? According to *Merriam-Webster.com*, civility is defined as "a polite act or expression," and "polite, reasonable and respectful behavior."

In practice, civility is more than that.

Civility in a workplace sets the tone for the culture. Civility in a home, educational facility, community or nation models the behavior that is expected and practiced. We've all been victims of mean-spirited individuals and comments.

Remember the saying, "Sticks and stones may break my bones, but words will never hurt me"? I don't agree.

My wonderful mom used that saying when someone would say or write something that was hurtful to me. Her kind spirit always helped encourage a mind-over-matter approach to get my spirit back on the high road. I have, however, witnessed situations where individuals have been marginalized and damaged through unkind words and actions they've not been able to overcome.

Today, social media has upped the ante. The world of bullying by texting, tweeting and online shaming creates cultures that are dishonest and abusive. These types of communications rate zero on the civility meter.

One result of this lack of civility is a get-even mind-set that divides people into hostile, opposing camps. We all can share stories of these behaviors and how they attack an individual's credibility, sometimes with lasting effects.

Companies especially understand the damage that can be done to reputations and financial earnings through false and malicious social media messages. They spend millions of dollars each year on crisis communications just to combat online falsehoods. The companies that have sustained long-term credibility understand the importance of the spoken or written word. They also know that how you treat your workforce, customers and one another sets the tone for success.

Maya Angelou informs us, "I've learned that people will forget what you said, people will forget what you did, but people will never forget how you made them feel."

Put another way, you'll always remember how you were treated.

As I already shared, my now 95-year-old mother would often use the sticks and stones saying. Although I tend to listen to my mom, I do believe words in today's world can be even more harmful than the traditional sticks and stones.

An often-tragic aspect of today's technology era is cyberbullying, which has resulted in an increase in teenage suicide. Through social media, it is possible for one or two people to anonymously carry out hate campaigns. I was very familiar with nicknames growing up, and some of them were mean-spirited. In today's world, name-calling has increased and become even more hurtful and visible.

To my mind, a key to civility is respect. Respectful individuals understand behavior and have a natural sensitivity to others. Their respect generates credibility and trust from others and establishes them as good role models. Their actions set the tone for civil discourse and a nurturing environment.

Respect for others is the soil that allows civility to grow.

We all know individuals who have this credibility and trust. They are routinely sought out to bridge differences between people and organizations.

Reverend Dr. Ronald Fowler is one of those men.

SuCCess

Reverend and Mrs. Ronald Fowler.
Courtesy of Fowler Family.

Rev. Fowler is the pastor laureate of the Arlington Church of God in Akron. His list of community involvement is robust and includes:

- Co-founder of the Love Akron Network
- Summit Education Initiative
- Akron Leadership Roundtable's This City Reads! Project
- Knight Foundation Community Advisory Committee
- Community Advisory Committee of Summit County Children's Services
- Center for Nonprofit Excellence–Akron
- National City Bank's Community Development Advisory Committee
- The University of Akron Student Discipline & Law Enforcement Policy Review Commission

Rev. Fowler understands and practices civility every minute of every day. He has high expectations of his congregation, friends, family and community. He is continually sought out to facilitate group discussions to address critical community challenges. He doesn't shy away from difficult tasks or people. He treats everyone with respect and, at the same time, sets a tone and example for positive interactions and decision-making.

This ingrained civility allows him to find the good in everyone and bring out the best in people. Rev. Fowler is not a name-caller or a mean-spirited individual. He empowers people, finds their strengths and knows how to listen.

In the most basic sense, he lives a life of service to others.

I have had the pleasure of working with Rev. Fowler on several community projects. We teamed up to address youth violence in our community. We co-chaired a Character Counts! initiative that promoted the six pillars of character: trustworthiness, respect, responsibility, fairness, caring and citizenship.

We co-chaired a This City Reads! literacy project and worked together on levies for our schools, Summit County Children's Services and much more. He is a consummate champion, encouraging people to come together regardless of their differences in gender, race, age and other trivial markers that can divide us.

In fact, Rev. Fowler was part of the nationally recognized Coming Together Project, an outgrowth of the yearlong, Pulitzer Prize-winning series on race relations published in 1993 by the *Akron Beacon Journal*, which was endorsed by former President Bill Clinton.

When people in Akron think of a person who embraces true civility, they think of Rev. Ronald Fowler. He created a lasting example for all of us. When you are in his presence, you are persuaded to be on your best behavior. He embraces a culture that promotes open, candid conversation, allowing for problems to be identified along with potential solutions.

Rev. Fowler's church services are inspiring, filled with positive energy and routine acts of kindness. I thought of Rev. Fowler recently when I was watching the funeral service for former President George H.W. Bush. President Bush had given a plaque to his minister that read, "Preach the gospel at all times, and if necessary use words." The message that actions speak louder than words is so true. Rev. Fowler's actions are always a model we can all follow.

Bernett Williams, a member of Rev. Fowler's congregation and vice president of External Affairs at Akron Children's Hospital, shared her thoughts on the man and his civility.

"Rev. Ronald J. Fowler modeled and taught civility well before it became a buzzword in our nation," she said. "Prior to his retirement as senior pastor of the Arlington Church of God, he gifted our church with one of his personal quotes:

> Lord make me
>
> Bigger than my foes.
>
> Wiser than your enemies.
>
> Stronger than my temptations
>
> and
>
> Better than before!

The quote sums up his character, which is deeply rooted in his faith and commitment to civility.

Rev. Fowler has a gift for simplifying what for many may seem difficult. He sums his philosophy up in one word: love. He shows love by his words and his deeds.

Bernett had the good fortune of serving in his congregation for almost 25 years. "I was drawn to his church as a young college student, partly due to his kind demeanor and loving heart," she said.

"He often preached about God's love and the expectation that we love and pray for one another—including those who do not love us."

"Love thy neighbor" is a way of life for Rev. Fowler. His actions show that civility can be maintained without sacrificing one's values. Disagreement and disappointment can be expressed without being uncivil.

In one innovative move, Rev. Fowler teamed up with Pastor Knute Larson, the now-retired senior pastor of The Chapel in Akron, to provide their separate congregations with new perspectives. These two men of God are phenomenal communicators and embrace civility in all their meaningful ministries. Within diversity, they found much common ground.

Rev. Fowler's church served many of Akron's inner-city residents. Rev. Larson's church was more popular with people from the suburbs. The two men bonded and broadened the Bible's teaching to reach their respective flocks. Their long-term relationship led to

Rev. Knute Larson (left) and Rev. Ronald Fowler. Courtesy of Love Akron Network.

collaborative projects, involvement in the Coming Together Project and increased awareness about meeting the needs of all the people in our community.

These two ministers led their congregations to civil and productive interactions, and their cooperative efforts became a national model for bringing people together.

Ron Fowler and Knute Larson are dear friends, and they teamed up to support our city's schools, neighborhoods and numerous other projects. Together, they were the driving force behind the first Love Akron prayer event and helped to establish this annual standing-room-only awards breakfast that honors servant leaders in the Akron area.

These two spiritual leaders are inspiring speakers who have long promoted civility and love for all people in our community.

How do you promote civility? Who are your role models for civil behavior? How do you think civility contributes to success?

Keys to Civility

- Be polite
- Show good manners
- Be respectful
- Be truthful
- Be understanding
- Be helpful

Chapter 4

Caring

IT'S NOT DIFFICULT TO find numerous examples of caring related to a children's hospital. Caring is evident daily among doctors, nurses, staff, volunteers, donors and others who seek to help our miracle children.

You'll meet one such person in a moment: Sarah Friebert, M.D., director of our Division of Palliative Care at Akron Children's Hospital. Dr. Friebert's caring spirit and the energy she gets from the children she serves translate into a compelling advocacy message she communicates daily.

You might ask, "How is caring an element of success?"

We all know people who believe in their own minds they are successful, but who are mean-spirited and care only about themselves. I've witnessed these individuals and know they can be very bright, driven and capable. My sense is their drive and desire for a successful financial bottom line clouds their outlook and blocks their caring spirit. Real success needs a caring element.

"We should underscore that caring isn't just a soft skill that can be pushed aside as the world becomes more strategic and accountability-driven," Dr. Friebert told me. "In fact, caring serves as one of the roots of all that is strategic and accountability-based in any organization."

People sense a caring spirit in a co-worker, boss and culture. A caring spirit is contagious and gets shared between people on a regular basis through words, smiles and actions. Caring offers hope in tough times. Caring offers excitement with opportunity. Caring offers assurance with uncertainties. Caring reduces stress and tensions. Caring generates energy in people that enables them to do their best.

Our best role models are caring individuals who know how to be present in the moment, listen and connect with people. Our best companies, ones that we admire, have a culture that truly cares about people: their workforce, customers and communities. These companies are involved through their connections and are enriched by them.

Caring counts, and it's evident wherever you look.

Like many people, I was blessed with caring parents and can share numerous life lessons they taught me and my siblings. I also encountered a phenomenal caring person on my first day of kindergarten, Mrs. Helen Bunts.

Kindergarten teacher Mrs. Helen Bunts.
Courtesy of Akron Public Schools.

Mrs. Bunts was a consummate gift to all her kindergarten students and established in them a foundation for a lifetime of continuous learning. Mrs. Bunts' classroom was interactive and a nonthreatening, creative environment. From day one, she knew everyone's name, greeted everyone with hugs and listened patiently to their stories.

She was a great storyteller, which led into a regular nap time in her room. She truly cared about every young life, and we cared about her. The bond was evident in our behavior: in our desire to learn, to be in her class, to be involved in the lessons and, of course, to roll out our towels for nap time.

I stayed in touch with Mrs. Bunts and reconnected with her 25 years after I was in her class when I returned as the Akron Children's Hospital CEO. She was the same caring person with a vast pool of class alumni whom she influenced with her enormous caring smile, hugs and spirit. I share with others in a speech I have given on role models that Mrs. Bunts, my kindergarten teacher, is one of my heroes and definitely a caring role model.

This brings us back to another care-oriented superhero, Dr. Friebert. Words will never capture the admiration people have for Dr. Friebert and her spirit of caring. From the minute you meet Sarah, you are embraced by her caring nature.

Palliative care represents the essence of caring. It is a holistic approach that adds an extra layer of support for children facing serious health conditions, as well as their families. The objective is to improve the quality of life of patients and families, and promote the prevention and relief of suffering by means of early identification, assessment and treatment of pain and other problems—physical, psychosocial and spiritual. More specifically, palliative care:

- Provides relief from pain and other distressing symptoms
- Integrates the psychological and spiritual aspects of patient care

- Seeks to enhance quality of life and may also positively influence the course of illness
- Is applicable early in the course of illness, in conjunction with other therapies intended to prolong life, such as chemotherapy or radiation therapy, and includes those investigations needed to better understand and manage distressing clinical complications
- Offers a support system to help families cope during a patient's illness and with their own stress and uncertainty
- Uses a team approach to address the needs of patients and their families, including bereavement counseling, if indicated
- Affirms life and regards dying as a normal process
- Intends neither to hasten nor postpone death
- Offers a support system to help patients live as actively as possible until death

Sarah Elizabeth Friebert, M.D. Courtesy of Akron Children's Hospital.

Dr. Friebert has added a human element to all these components of palliative care and is recognized internationally for her pioneering work in this specialized area of medicine. She is loved by her patients, families, co-workers and our ancillary caregivers.

She bonds with patients through house calls, stories, hospitalizations, birthdays, graduations, memorials and trusted conversations. She listens and learns about hopes, fears and new realities that are thrust onto patients and families. She assists in realizing dreams and creating lasting life legacies.

In addition, she cares about the caregivers and the stress that impacts their lives. She has organized programs for these men and women through her caring spirit. I've seen firsthand that spirit in action. She empowers her team and colleagues with her passion.

Dr. Friebert's caring spirit made a significant difference to a young girl named Cassidy.

Cassidy was an 11-year-old who had a dream of being an artist. In her mind, she saw children and others smiling at her paintings and reading meaning into the shapes, colors and scenes she would put on a blank canvas. She dreamed about bringing that canvas to life with her passion and skill.

Cassidy's dream was detoured when she was diagnosed with a serious tumor. The medical team did their very best, and Cassidy's attitude and spirit provided them with extra incentive and energy. She was a gift to all the lives she touched.

"She was actually very creative," Dr. Friebert said. "She painted, sketched, wrote stories and poems. She was determined to do something with her time. She didn't just want to sit there."

Her dream never changed as she fought a debilitating cancer that left the left side of her body paralyzed in her fight for life. She had, in her hospitalization, become acquainted with the palliative care team, a collaborative group of physicians, nurses, therapists, social workers and others who provide support to patients. The patient they were now assisting was Cassidy as she and her family prepared for her death.

Success

Cassidy, being an artist, saw the team from an artist's perspective. In her mind, "palliative care" became "palette of care." The team was the painter's palette, and she was the brush. She was able to dip into the various paint colors whether they be physicians, nurses, music therapists or others to create her vision. Cassidy painted a picture of an artist's palette in her mind. A beautiful oasis, palm tree and shining sun created by the team ... a true palette of care.

Cassidy painted this beautiful scene and presented it to the palliative care team before she died.

"I actually paid her for the picture so she could consider herself to be a famous artist," Dr. Friebert said. "And her picture is the main inspiration behind our calling the team 'A Palette of Care.'"

"Palette of Care" painting by Cassidy Jackson. Courtesy of Akron Children's Hospital.

The hospital copyrighted Cassidy's artwork and helped her realize her dream of being an artist whose work would be seen by others around the world. All national presentations made by our palliative care team start with Cassidy's painting. Caring made a difference and established a legacy.

Through Dr. Friebert's dedicated efforts, she developed a vision for a world-class service that would be known for its quality, human touch, family focus and caring. Her work quickly established a standard of excellence and, despite the challenges of palliative care not being reimbursed by insurance companies, she attracted support from numerous sources.

Dr. Friebert also holds an endowed chair in palliative care. Several caring families were inspired by her spirit and created and endowed the chair that carries her name, the Sarah Elizabeth Friebert, M.D. Leadership Chair in Pediatric Palliative Care. It was the first such chair in the United States. The generous individuals who made the chair possible were Eileen Burg, Mark and Cathy Clark, and Sandra Haslinger and Family.

Dr. Friebert also led the pioneering effort to establish our country's second fellowship program for graduating medical residents who want to specialize in pediatric palliative care. The fellowship continues to grow and currently takes two candidates each year into the program.

Dr. Friebert received the "Children's Miracle Achievement Award" in 2009 from the Children's Miracle Network. This was the first time pediatric palliative care was recognized on the national stage. Personally, Sarah is not about awards. She prefers to use the recognition to educate people and organizations about the importance of providing this humane and caring approach to children and families facing chronic and terminal diagnoses.

In her precious spare time, Sarah organizes events to stay in touch with the families she's cared for over the years. She has served as president of the Akron Children's Hospital medical staff; she's involved with our community's opioid initiative; she helped establish Schwartz Center Rounds at our hospital, which give a platform for providers to share experiences, process stressful situations and improve communication; and she formed a support program to address provider burnout.

This phenomenal individual truly cares, and that spirit is inspiring to anyone who interacts with her.

The success these individuals have achieved in enriching the lives of others is definitely tied to their caring spirit. Their success is defined in the achievement of others. As Dr. Friebert said, caring is the root—the foundation of any successful organization.

Keys to Caring

- Show concern for others
- Embrace a daily act of kindness
- Model humanitarian behavior
- Celebrate others' good deeds
- Nurture

Chapter 5
Community

PEOPLE WHO LEAD SUCCESSFUL initiatives are those who can connect and identify with a sense of community. These people get to know all sectors of a community and its citizens. Community-focused men and women hear the stories from neighborhoods, churches and schools. By tapping into the pulse of people, they understand the issues that need to be addressed.

Akron, Ohio, has been blessed with a wealth of leaders in its history, many of whom could be mentioned here. Four inspiring individuals stand out, not only for their leadership but for their integrity: John S. Knight, Dorothy Jackson, David Lieberth and George Knepper.

The standards are high. A community-focused leader creates an informal and engaged citizenship, advancing a better quality of life for all. Community pride rises around the effort put forward by each community champion. This pride is absorbed by citizens in their homes, workplaces, churches, neighborhoods and more. Success is a by-product of that community pride.

Brothers John S. (Jack) and James L. (Jim) Knight developed a newspaper empire that began in their hometown of Akron. Jack Knight became one of the world's most renowned journalists, interacting with U.S. presidents and international dignitaries. His editorials were thoughtful, and the powerful words in those messages—truth, equality, liberty—are relevant today.

SUCCESS

As *Akron Beacon Journal* editor, Knight was awarded the 1968 Pulitzer Prize for Editorial Writing, a rare honor for any journalist.

Jack Knight, for all his success, always remembered his community and the communities where he and his brother expanded their business through acquisitions and a merger with Ridder Newspapers in 1974.

"Jack and Jim Knight were astonishingly successful, focusing on journalism excellence and service to community," said Alberto Ibarguen, president, CEO and trustee of the Knight Foundation. "That's how they created, in their day, the biggest newspaper company in America ... at a time when newspapers were at the core of all news.

"When they created a foundation, they gave direction by saying what they cared about, journalism and communities, but were not prescriptive. They explicitly wanted future trustees to decide how the foundation would remain relevant over time," Ibarguen continued. "By focusing on the way the brothers ran their newspapers and taking seriously their donor intent, the Knight Foundation continues to contribute to democracy in America."

At its height, the Knight Ridder enterprise owned a newspaper in 28 cities, along with other media properties. During the last decades of the 20th century, the Knight Ridder Newspapers' empire was the nation's largest in terms of circulation and was among the most respected media organizations in the world.

"The Knight brothers believed local communities were the genius of American democracy," Ibarguen said. Ibarguen is former publisher of the *Miami Herald* and the Spanish-language *El Nuevo Herald*. "They structured their newspaper company so that each Knight newspaper would best represent the different interests and opportunities of the many communities they served. They promoted our democracy by helping to create and inspire informed and engaged citizens so that, in Jack Knight's words, 'the people might pursue their true interests.'"

Brothers Jack (left) and Jim Knight. Courtesy of the Knight Foundation.

But Jack Knight didn't start with an empire. He started with the *Akron Beacon Journal*, inherited from his father, C.L. Knight, in 1933, the middle of the Great Depression. He often had to pay employees with tokens they could take to local merchants—basically IOUs. He realized early that a newspaper had to be financially strong to be independent.

"Unless a newspaper is profitable, how the hell do you have any liberty?" Knight once told an editor's spouse, as recounted in a tribute by Clark Hoyt, a former Knight Ridder Washington Bureau chief. "I'm free. Nobody puts pressure on me."

Knight's own bottom line, however, was his oft-quoted statement: "A typewriter means more to a newspaper than an adding machine."

Hoyt wrote that when Knight took his company public in 1969, he had only one meeting with stock market analysts. He told them, "Ladies and gentlemen, I do not intend to become your prisoner."

SUCCESS

Jack Knight's papers always had a community focus in their coverage that was factual and enlightening. Knight's goal was to inform and engage the readers. He promoted people and communities through his news and helped them understand, as one editor said, "not necessarily what to think but what to think about."

One Knight quote that hung in the *Beacon Journal* newsroom long after his death spoke to his sense of community. "I don't care who runs Akron," he once wrote, "as long as somebody does."

Strong editorials were a foundation of his community involvement. He once came across a fluffy editorial in the *Akron Beacon Journal* that came to no conclusion and offered no solution to a local issue. He sent a starchy, sarcastic note to the page editor: "A bold stand, sir!"

Knight never asked reporters or editors about their politics or their beliefs. His simple mantra—"Get the truth and print it"—was

Jack Knight. Courtesy of the Knight Foundation.

the hallmark of a leader, Hoyt said, that "you would go through a wall for."

Jack Knight always remembered that his enormous success came through the communities where his papers were sold. He was a man of influence and understood the responsibilities that came with that leadership role. He spoke the truth and held people accountable to their spoken word and responsibilities.

I first heard the Knight name when I was a paperboy delivering Knight's hometown signature paper, the *Akron Beacon Journal*. In my collegiate years, I met Mr. Knight when I was president of The University of Akron Student Council and introduced him when he spoke to a student gathering about the Vietnam conflict. When I returned to Akron in 1979, I came into contact with Mr. Knight at a local country club, and he wished me well in my new role.

In my position at Akron Children's Hospital, I soon witnessed the impact of the foundation he and his brother had established. Jack Knight died in 1981, and his brother passed away in 1991. Today I have the honor of serving on the Knight Foundation Board based in Miami, Florida. The foundation has assets of over $2 billion and supports the cities where the Knight Ridder Newspapers thrived.

There are eight major cities (Akron, Ohio; Miami, Fla.; Detroit, Mich.; Philadelphia, Pa.; Macon, Ga.; San Jose, Calif.; St. Paul, Minn;. Charlotte, N.C.) where the foundation places community-based program directors. There are another 18 cities (Aberdeen, S.D.; Biloxi, Miss.; Boulder, Colo.; Bradenton, Fla.; Columbia, S.C.; Columbus, Ga.; Duluth, Minn.; Ft. Wayne, Ind.; Gary, Ind.; Grand Forks, N.D.; Lexington, Ky.; Long Beach, Calif.; Milledgeville, Ga.; Myrtle Beach, S.C.; Palm Beach County, Fla.; State College, Penn.; Tallahassee, Fla.; and Wichita, Kan.) also eligible for foundation funding.

Through his role with the Knight Foundation, Ibarguen sees both the lasting influence and the hometown values of the Knights.

"In their day, Jack and Jim Knight were on top of the world. They knew leaders across the country and influenced thought by having the largest newspaper company in America. If there had been a Forbes list, they might have been on it. But they never lost sight of home.

"Jack Knight lived in Akron all his life and developed special love for Detroit and Miami. Jim Knight raised his family in Miami and moved to Charlotte toward the end of his life. Neither one of them forgot community values; both of them thrived on active engagement where they lived and worked. They were American news moguls, for sure," Ibarguen said, "but they never stopped being home towners."

The Knight Foundation continues to invest in journalism, in the arts and in the success of cities where brothers John S. and James L. Knight once published newspapers. The goal is to foster informed and engaged communities, which trustees believe are essential for a healthy democracy. The Knights created a lasting legacy that promotes communities and the people in those communities.

Even though Knight Ridder Newspapers were sold 25 years after Jack Knight died, the Knight Foundation today is thriving and keeping alive the brothers' love of communities, journalism and art.

In 1979, I met another genuine community champion. Dorothy O. Jackson was known then and is still referred to in a biographical sketch as the Akron community's "goodwill ambassador."

For almost 20 years, Jackson served as deputy mayor of the city, becoming the first African-American woman to serve in an Akron mayor's cabinet. Jackson retired in June 2003 but had no plans to give up her community activism.

Dorothy was born in east Akron, and her father worked at the Goodyear Tire and Rubber Co. She graduated from Akron's East High School and Actual Business College. She attended Kent State University and The University of Akron.

In 1956, Dorothy went to work at Goodwill Industries, where she taught job skills to physically and mentally challenged people.

"I loved training handicapped people, teaching them skills and taking them on educational field trips," Jackson told David Lieberth

Dorothy Jackson. Courtesy of Bruce Ford, City of Akron.

(another community asset) in a taped interview. "I always say that Goodwill is the best school I ever went to."

Some of those who needed the skills training were deaf. In order to communicate, Jackson began on her own learning American Sign Language. Then, with a scholarship, Dorothy attended Gallaudet College, a college for the deaf in Washington, D.C., and became fluent in sign language. Since then, she has served as a volunteer interpreter for the deaf at churches and community activities.

Jackson left Goodwill in 1968 and joined the Akron Metropolitan Housing Authority (AMHA). As human services administrator, she directed award-winning service programs for the 20,000 residents of the AMHA.

Those programs—including day care, summer youth and teacher programs, Head Start centers, programming for seniors, literacy and homemaker training—were nationally recognized and became national models.

"The manual I wrote (about programming) is still used by HUD (the U.S. Department of Housing and Urban Development)," she said.

Mayor Tom Sawyer appointed Jackson deputy mayor for Intergovernmental Relations in 1984. Jackson said it was hard to leave AMHA.

"I feel like I touched those families. And they touched me," she said.

Jackson had doubts that she could even handle the deputy mayor's job. She asked for advice—and prayers—from her friend the Rev. Ronald Fowler.

"Can you help more people by being in the mayor's office?" Fowler asked. Jackson said she could.

"Then apply," Fowler counseled.

Jackson applied on the last day the city was taking applications. She got the job, even though other applicants seemed, on paper, to have more education and experience. It was an insightful decision by Mayor Sawyer.

Dorothy flourished in the office and continued her city service with Mayor Donald Plusquellic as his government's liaison to a wide range of civic and community groups.

Under Plusquellic, Jackson served on local, state and national boards and committees. She was a trustee for Akron General Medical Center and chaired the United Way/Red Cross Partnership Council. She also played a role at Northeastern Educational Television of Ohio and the National Retirement Communities for the Church of God. She served on the advisory committees of National City Bank and the Junior League of Akron.

Although retired, Jackson continues to serve as interpreter for the deaf at Arlington Church of God and as a member of the National Registry of Professional Interpreters and Translators, the

Life Membership Committee of NAACP, the National Caucus on the Black Aged and the Senior Citizens Advisory Council.

Jackson has won many awards over her decades of service to the community, including the Bert A. Polsky Humanitarian Award, the Ohio Black Women's Leadership Caucus Rosa Parks Award, United Way's Distinguished Service Award and the Urban League's Community Service Award. She has also been inducted into the Ohio Women's Hall of Fame. A 28-unit handicapped housing development in Akron was named Dorothy O. Jackson Terrace in her honor. The Jewish National Fund named a park in Kiryat Ekron, Israel, after her.

Dorothy routinely was the spokesperson for the community. She championed the All-American City designation and was the city ambassador on a mission to Israel. She advocated for Akron's elderly, homeless and underprivileged.

In her early professional career, she was a nursing assistant at Akron Children's Hospital and, at that time, developed an unbreakable bond with the community's young children. She continuously answered the call from entities reaching out to serve the community's children.

She also loved cooking. Her baking skills came from her mother.

"The way I remember my early life is three F's," she said. "Family, food and fun, and in that order."

Even as a child in east Akron, the youngest of seven children, she recalls the family garden. "We always had food, so everyone came to our house."

To connect with people and community, her artistry in the kitchen often was the first welcoming card. I always enjoy the story of her writing a cookbook.

Dorothy was dating a young man who confessed that he did not know how to cook. For a Christmas gift, Dorothy wrote a cookbook for him titled *How to Boil Water and Other Things Too Good to Miss*. She soon discovered her colleagues at work wanted a copy and, when she had the book bound, the people at the print shop wanted

SuCCess

a copy, too. She inherited the love of cooking from her mother and then shared her love and recipes with the greater Akron community.

Dorothy embraced this wide stage for advocacy for all citizens. Her leadership was connected to a community message, and her phenomenal credibility was based on her success on community-based initiatives.

I have witnessed firsthand her effective leadership and count her as a friend and influence. Dorothy is a gift to the Akron community. The organization Love Akron honored Dorothy Jackson in 2016 as a role model and champion for the community.

Her caring and optimism are reflected in a saying she remembers from her father, William, as a way to help others overcome hard times. "Dot," he would say, "anybody can fall, but nobody has to wallow."

Community was Dorothy Jackson's passion as a leader, and she successfully enriched the lives of everyone she touched.

Another consummate community champion is a person I've already mentioned when discussing other phenomenal people and role models. David Lieberth is a man for all seasons and one with enormous credibility in the Akron community.

He has been one of the most recognized voices in greater Akron for five decades. He spent 35 years in the private sector—as a media reporter and news director, and as a practicing lawyer and mediator for 25 years.

As a broadcaster, he earned a reputation as one of northeast Ohio's most skillful, objective and dynamic communicators. Dave also has been one of Summit County's most respected attorneys. For 10 years, Dave was listed among the "Best Lawyers in America" in Matrimonial Law. He served as Akron's deputy mayor and the mayor's chief of staff from 2002 to 2012.

I first met Dave when we were students at The University of Akron. He was active in student organizations and became the voice of our campus radio station. We served together on student government and were involved in numerous university activities, groups

Dave Lieberth. Courtesy of Bruce Ford, City of Akron.

and student engagement projects. Dave early on showed skill in organizing and staging events. He was and is a gifted communicator and production planner. He's always said if you're going to stage an event, "Do it big or go home."

Dave's belief in our community led him to learn more about local history. He became active in the historical society and preservation society. He directed the monumental *Marking of the Trail of the Portage Path*, completed in 2001. He utilized his production skills to film local historians and capture their stories and knowledge. A list of his major productions includes:

- Producer, two television documentaries for PBS 45/49, *Inventive. Industrious. Inspired*, a history of Akron (2000), which was honored by the Columbus International Film Festival; and *Reinventing Akron: Stories of a Generation* (2001).

SuCCess

- Director, Akron's 175th anniversary celebration (2000), producer of more than 40 commemorative events.
- Producer and principal writer, All-American City Award, National Civic League (1995 and 2008).
- Producer, Opening Ceremonies, John S. Knight Center dedication (1994).
- Producer, Opening Ceremonies, Canal Park Stadium dedication (1997).
- Producer, Inventure Place Groundbreaking Ceremonies (1993) and Dedication Ceremonies (1995).
- Producer and principal writer, Induction Ceremonies, National Inventors Hall of Fame (1990–1996).
- Producer for the reveal of the 1950 Time Capsule, Perkins Mansion, September 2000.
- Moderator, President Bill Clinton's first Town Meeting on Race, December 1997, sponsored by the White House, carried on C-SPAN TV.
- Moderator, first statewide roundtable on "Judicial Impartiality," convened by the Chief Justice, Ohio Supreme Court (2003).
- Moderator, statewide forums on families and children, Supreme Court of Ohio Judicial College (2007, 2008).
- Producer, principal writer and narrator, LeBron James Homecoming, InfoCision Stadium, August 2014.
- Producer and principal writer, LeBron James NBA Championship, Lock 3 (2016).

Dave has been the master of ceremonies for numerous events. The community's Polsky Humanitarian Award, which is presented by the Akron Community Foundation, connected with Dave for 37 years to produce the annual award ceremony to honor a deserving individual. Dave conducted the interviews, developed a narrative and produced a video that captured the essence of each individual. He also emceed the opening of hometown basketball superstar LeBron James' I PROMISE School in August 2018.

Dave was instrumental in Akron's Coming Together diversity project being recognized nationally, drawing the attention of former President Bill Clinton. The project grew from a Pulitzer Prize-winning series by the *Akron Beacon Journal*.

He led a successful community contingent in competition to be designated an All-American City.

In one ongoing contribution, Dave was a founder of the Leadership Akron program. He believed it was important to actively promote leadership development, to invest in the city's talent and then retain that talent. The program showcases the community, discusses opportunities for improvement, connects participants with areas of interest and builds community pride and collaboration. Participants learn how to lead in community and civic life through membership on local boards and other service projects.

A Leadership Akron class of approximately 35 individuals from the community is selected annually for the year-long program. By the end of 2018, there had been 35 leadership classes with 1,357 graduates in its three programs. Dave was honored by Leadership Akron in 2012 when it instituted the David Lieberth Leadership Akron Award of Excellence.

Dave's love of Akron led the mayor to recruit him as a deputy mayor in 2002, to focus on bringing Downtown Akron alive. An area known as Lock 3—a stop on the old Ohio Erie Canal—became the stage for Dave to bring people downtown for entertainment, family gatherings, holiday celebrations and more.

A group known as Downtown Akron Partnership became a key collaborative for downtown investment and a family-friendly atmosphere. Dave initiated the Summer Arts Experience for high school students. He founded the Heinz Poll Summer Dance Festival and continues to manage its 12th season, including the free Sunday summer concerts by the Akron Symphony.

SuCCess

Much more can be attributed to Dave's pride and belief in his hometown and the people of Akron. He once put his commitment into words during a commencement speech to graduates at Hoban High School.

"When we are at our best of being unselfish," he told the graduates, "when we give to others through leading lives of service, the return on our investment of the time we give and share with others are the memories that last. Many of you have already learned that life can be hard. Life can seem unfair. But the antidote can be unselfish service to others. It rounds the sharp edges on our lives."

Dave Lieberth is a community champion who has lived these words through his actions.

A fourth champion of my hometown community was a University of Akron history professor, the late Dr. George Knepper.

George Knepper. Courtesy of The University of Akron.

47

Knepper did more than teach in the classroom. He brought the past to life in his lectures, writings and stories. He believed the past should be respected and remembered for the people who came before us and the lessons they offered through their lives. He knew the past always paves the road to the future.

In frequent lectures around the Akron area, Knepper stressed the historic importance of this community, in social progress, innovation, political influence and its continual rebirth—from Native American portage trail, to frontier farming and settlement, to busy port on the Ohio Erie Canal, to the birth of the nation's rubber industry and to the technological, knowledge-based economy that followed.

Dave Lieberth recalls a comment about Knepper made by the late business and civic leader William Giermann, when Knepper gave one of his many lectures to Leadership Akron.

"Bill Giermann used to say that when George spoke, you got the feeling that whatever he was talking about, whether it was 1960 or 1860, he was in the back of the room while it was going on," Lieberth told me.

These lessons of the past prove beneficial as a foundation for the present. Knowledge of community, in George's mind, was an enormous resource for all leaders, pointing to future success in their endeavors.

When George graduated from Buchtel High School he told his friends that after his military service (it was 1943) he was going to college, to what became The University of Akron, instead of joining them at one of the rubber companies.

"They thought I was crazy," he said. "They said, 'not only will you have to pay for college, you'll miss the four years' of salary you could have made.'"

It turned out to be a good decision. George Knepper served the university from 1948 to 1992, and served the Akron community his whole life, until his death in 2018 at age 92.

In addition to teaching, Knepper was an administrator, including dean of the Buchtel College of Arts and Sciences; a Fulbright

SuCCess

Fellow at the University of London; researcher of the materials that became the University (of Akron) Archives; president of the Summit County Historical Society, the Ohio Historical Society and the Ohio Academy of History; and author of eight books, including the popular and award-winning *Ohio and Its People*.

Knepper produced a compilation of community stories and pictures in a book he published in 1980–81, *Akron: City at the Summit*, which is now in its third printing. The book captures the history of a community that became Akron, Ohio. In it, the pictures and narrative come together to describe the components that formed this community. The stories that comprise the book link directly to Akron of the 21st century and create ownership of community in its readers.

Jack Knight, Dorothy Jackson, Dave Lieberth and George Knepper brought pride in community to everyone they engaged. They were admired and sought-after leaders because of their knowledge and willingness to share it with others. They proudly built bridges between people and organizations, and from the past to the future, and they did so in a fashion that was transformational.

They understood a community's past always paves the road to the future. These were leaders who boosted the greater Akron community while becoming a valued part of its history.

How do you connect with community? What are your stories? What people come to your mind as those who recognized no boundaries or who overcame obstacles in order to champion their community?

Keys to Community

- Promote community investment
- Be involved with community organizations
- Attend community events
- Be an active community citizen
- Know your community's history and challenges

Chapter 6
Collaboration

THE CONCEPT OF TEAMWORK is perhaps most obvious in the world of sports. It is the key to success and championship performance. Teamwork is also a major factor in any organization's success, creating a just and efficient culture in the workplace. Collaboration elevates a team or company to a higher level of performance.

The Akron Children's Hospital story I shared earlier is a wonderful example of the power of collaboration. Two groups of women affiliated with two different churches simultaneously had the idea to form a nursery to serve Akron families. When the groups discovered they had the same idea, they mutually agreed to collaborate.

Collaboration enabled them to create an even more compelling message to help Akron's children and families. They avoided the selfish approach of arguing over who originated the idea. That dispute would have created a negative environment and detracted from a worthwhile ideal. The friendly collaboration led to the creation of the Mary Day Nursery, forerunner to what is now Akron Children's Hospital. It's an unforgettable lesson about the power of collaboration.

Put simply, collaboration can be defined as two or more organizations or individuals working together toward a common goal.

Workplace expert Carol Kinsey Goman crafts speeches and seminars around collaborative leadership. In an article on this topic, she offers sound advice, "Collaboration is not a nice-to-have organizational philosophy. It is an essential ingredient for an organization's survival and success."

How do you, as a leader, advance a dream? What is the vision of the organization and people you're privileged to serve? There are many ways to make the impossible possible, but how do you motivate people to follow your lead?

We've all heard the phrase, "There's no 'I' in team." Duke University basketball coach Mike Krzyzewski, the legendary Coach K, talks about the hand being much more effective when all five digits are in sync.

The importance of teamwork has been proven time after time. High-performing teams have individual members who are empowered and understand their role. This is as true in health care as it is in sports, but it requires empowering the patient to be an integral member of the care team.

Leaders know the importance of team and the power of collaboration. Leaders know they cannot be loners, and they know they must have faith in their teams. Leaders obviously need to invest in people and support continuous learning, including having the opportunity to learn from each other through collaboration. Empowerment will result in pride, ownership, innovation, satisfaction and true value.

We have all been captivated by the stories of great storytellers. Sharing collaborative experiences that bring reality to the various situations we face in our daily lives can assist in empowering people. I was also influenced by leaders who were good storytellers and who used this skill to inform, engage and create excitement about working together.

As noted in my book *Leadership*, storytelling "influences us every day in the products we buy, the causes we support and the careers we choose."

Naturally, storytelling is influential within an organization. According to Robert McKee, an author, lecturer and consultant, "Storytelling is the most powerful way to put ideas into the world today."

Who are the storytellers or leaders who have influenced you? What types of stories have had the most impact? What has been your experience in storytelling?

I've personally seen how collaboration can open the door to transformational initiatives. Successful leaders promote collaboration and understand its benefits. Two individuals I know who have modeled the spirit of collaboration are Terry Mulligan and Father Rick Frechette.

Terry Mulligan is my dear friend. I've witnessed his enormous leadership skills in action as a valuable health care leader. He's a gifted collaborator, and he knows how to gather people around an opportunity to motivate them to work together in achieving a worthwhile goal.

Terry's story about his early high school experience illustrates this basic lesson. As a student enrolled in a new school, he didn't know anyone, but he enjoyed football and was a talented athlete. When he tried out for the team, he found they had a new coach, Chuck Kelly. The team was coming off a very poor season the previous year, and success seemed like a fleeting goal.

Coach Kelly saw something more valuable than just athletic talent in Terry. He talked with him about using his effort, attitude and confidence to unite the team. Coach Kelly and Terry agreed to work together to achieve a turnaround for their team.

The team went on to have a championship season that year, and Terry was offered a scholarship to the University of Iowa. As a defensive end for the Hawkeyes, he received varsity letters for football in 1964, 1965 and 1966, before graduating and joining the U.S. Army.

Chuck Lauer, late publisher of the magazine *Modern Healthcare,* was a close friend of Terry's, and he wrote an article about the lessons Terry learned during his military service. Titled "Don't Mail It In," the article illustrates the importance of personal effort and its connection to success.

Chuck captured the essence of his dear friend in several of his writings. Together, Chuck and Terry mentored numerous others in the art of achieving success.

Chuck encouraged me to write my first book, and he wrote the foreword to *Leadership* shortly before he died. He was a gifted writer who could share valuable life lessons through his words and actions.

At Chuck's funeral, Terry gave the eulogy. He captured the spirit of the man who left a lasting legacy of service and excellence through his editorials and other writings. These two men brought out the best in each other, and they collaborated to benefit the lives of many others.

Following his military service, Terry worked for the American Hospital Supply Company, which later merged with Baxter

Chuck S. Lauer, 2013. Courtesy of *Modern Healthcare*.

International, Inc. Terry was an influential executive and had a stellar 26-year career with the company.

I met Terry in the 1980s and was immediately impressed by his knowledge of people and his ability to bring them together, a skill he honed during his athletic and military experiences. He set the table for members of the Baxter team to meet with pediatric hospital representatives from around the nation to collaborate on ways to improve their revenue cycles and supply chain management processes. He brought strangers together, identified a common goal and established positive, productive conversations.

Vern Loucks, CEO of Baxter during Terry's tenure, remains impressed. "Terry is perhaps the most positive and loyal individual I've known, EVER!" Loucks told me. "His positivity goes a long way toward gaining the will and collaboration of his team to achieve complex, worthy goals. With this and his commitment to accomplish, he weaves a very compelling and embraceable web of positive expectation and reward by his team that does not break down."

Loucks is himself a successful business and civic leader, and he credits Terry with instilling a "killer instinct" within his team, "through an intense collaborative desire to succeed. Terry always knew his team was well-informed, understood the goal and never embraced quit" as a possibility.

Collaboration is a positive attitude that successful leaders cultivate.

Terry uses his collaborative skills not only in his work. He has also served as president of the University of Iowa's Alumni Association and as a board member for the Children's Miracle Network and countless other organizations. He has been routinely sought after to advise start-up companies about how to network with like-minded partners and identify collaboration opportunities for entrepreneurs.

A striking example of this talent is evident in the work Terry did for a company called MedAssets, Inc. He was an early resource for the company's founder, John Bardis. Terry assisted John by identifying initial contacts and board members. He also assembled an advisory group of people with different backgrounds and areas of expertise who responded to Terry's collaborative agenda and vision.

Terry will tell you he benefitted from great mentors like Vern Loucks before becoming a mentor himself. Terry's leadership skills are unsurpassed. His belief in the power of collaboration and his faith in people are the keys to his exemplary professional career.

Terry and his wife, Susan, have been married for 50 years and have a beautiful family. They are generous philanthropists, and he continues to share his collaborative ideas with his retired friends, as well as aspiring young men and women.

Another of my collaborative heroes is Father Richard Frechette, a Roman Catholic priest and practicing physician. Rick's missionary work brought him to Haiti 31 years ago. His collaborative spirit and healing nature have been gifts to the people of that country.

Terry Mulligan. Courtesy of the University of Iowa.

He's lived through earthquakes, epidemics and civil unrest and remains a man of faith who believes in the goodness of people. He has the skills to bring people together in a culture of collaboration working toward a greater goal. He has shown regularly that a group can achieve what no one person can on their own, especially important in a nation with constant challenges and limited resources.

When Father Rick assessed the situation in Haiti, he quickly concluded the children of Port-au-Prince had a great need for medical services. He also knew he would need the help of numerous people and organizations to begin meeting that need. He developed the idea of building a children's hospital and found a way to make that idea a reality—and thus St. Damien Pediatric Hospital was born.

Father Rick, through his talent for collaboration, ministry, storytelling and hard work, enlisted people and organizations to help him build a simple hospital structure. Funds for the building

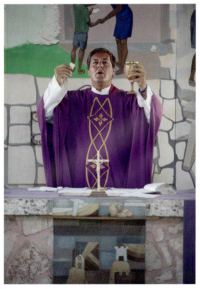

Father Rick Frechette. Courtesy of Ted Stevens.

came from the various foundations, individuals and enterprises that wanted to be part of his vision to help Haiti's children.

Initial services at the hospital were rudimentary, but Father Rick was not yet satisfied. He had a vision to create a facility that would employ local people who could help it grow.

Collaboration was the natural foundation. His team opened a bakery that offered jobs to people who made bread for the hospital. They also sold their bread in the community. The team started a facility repair operation that employed Haitians who were trained to maintain the hospital's infrastructure and equipment. They developed the expertise to service cars and were able to charge competitive rates for their work.

The ecosystem Father Rick was developing grew to include a poultry farm, vegetable garden, fish hatchery, furniture shop, clothing store and a solar energy plant. This cooperative enterprise now includes the children's hospital, a separate rehabilitation hospital, an elementary and secondary school, a dorm facility for students and a visitor complex.

This complex is used by the caregivers who come from around the world to collaborate under the direction of Father Rick and enhance the clinical programs available to the children.

The emergency room facility and capabilities have been upgraded, as have the intensive care unit and operating rooms. Teams of medical professionals are training Haitian caregivers, offering internships and technology support. Open heart surgical procedures to correct congenital heart defects, for example, can now be performed at St. Damien's. A partnership with Rotary International has been an indispensable ingredient in this transformation.

The St. Damien's team has also reached out when natural disasters have befallen Haiti. The positive response is an example of and tribute to the power of collaboration.

Father Rick's vision remains exciting and embraces everyone who is willing to come to the table. Akron Children's providers Dr. Jeff Kempf, a pediatric emergency physician and director of the

Office of Pediatric Global Health, and his wife, Dr. Ellen Kempf, a pediatrician, have traveled to St. Damien's over a dozen times. Although semiretired, they remain part of the collaboration and the phenomenal advancements that are benefitting Haitian children.

"Father Rick inspired us to come and serve at St. Damien's," Dr. Jeff Kempf said. "He has reminded us that we each have a finite number of heartbeats and we should ask ourselves, what is our heart beating for?"

Terry Mulligan and Father Rick Frechette are both true gifts to those who interact with them. They have successful life experiences and are admired and trusted leaders. Their spirit of collaboration is a vital element of their leadership.

Another example of collaboration that benefits children in Akron and beyond is a program known as Solutions for Patient Safety (SPS). In 2008, the children's hospitals in Ohio met to discuss ways to advance quality services in their hospitals. Dr. Uma Kotagal, a neonatologist and currently the executive leader of Population and Community Health and a Senior Fellow at Cincinnati Children's Hospital Medical Center, facilitated that first meeting.

Dr. Kotagal is a highly respected international champion for patient safety. Based on her vision, Ohio's eight children's hospitals decided they should learn from each other and share information and outcomes on their quality initiatives rather than compete on patient safety results. Jim Anderson, former CEO of Cincinnati Children's Hospital, said at the time, "We will compete on execution, but we will not compete on ideas." Thus, the concept of "all teach, all learn" was implemented.

Quality representatives from the hospitals discussed the philosophy of zero harm, evaluated current patient outcomes and began open discussions. Negative outcomes in patient safety and quality were identified and discussed by clinicians. Improvement plans were developed, tested and shared among the eight hospitals. Parental input was also solicited, and a spirit of true collaboration was embraced.

SuCCess

Uma R. Kotagal, MBBs, MSc. Courtesy of Uma Kotagal.

Soon, positive results were realized, and successful best-practice patient treatment bundles were instituted across all hospitals. Collaboration and quality became a topic of discussion at national meetings.

Health care was under pressure to do better, following reports such as the Institute of Medicine's "To Err is Human," which illustrated how the complexity of hospital systems could prevent safe care from occurring. Leaders from Ohio's children's hospitals worked with industry experts from high reliability organizations (HROs) to bring a culture of safety and reliability into health care. By learning from the nuclear power, aviation and other high-risk industries already using HRO principles to mitigate risks, hospital leaders, their governing boards and clinical staff were able to improve their systems for the betterment of their patients.

In fact, at our first Ohio Children's Hospital Patient Safety Forum, Richard Grigg, a nuclear engineer and chairman of Akron Children's board of directors, spoke up when some questioned the feasibility of achieving zero harm and wondered if we could truly collaborate. Dick responded that the question we should have been asking was how we can *NOT* afford to do this work. Having lost a family member due to a medical error, Dick knew we could and should do better.

Companies in Ohio joined the SPS team. Through a high level of collaboration, we reduced harm to patients, and the journey to zero harm was underway. Children's hospitals around the country expressed their interest in joining the network, and the collaborative grew.

Ten years after that initial meeting, there are more than 135 children's hospitals participating in the SPS network sharing patient safety protocols. The improved quality processes have resulted in a measurable effect with harmful outcomes avoided for more than 12,700 children.

The collaborative also shares information on staff safety and is working to address accidents and other challenges faced by our caregivers. These are programs that promote the formation of HROs. The Joint Commission and the National Quality Forum honored the SPS network with their prestigious John M. Eisenberg Patient Safety and Quality Award in 2018, which recognizes major achievements of individuals and organizations that improve patient safety and health care quality.

Collaboration among the executive and clinical leaders of the hospitals is a perfect example of the power of working together. The benefit of this collaborative is not in the awards, but in enriching the lives of children.

What examples of collaboration have you witnessed? What collaborative initiatives have you been involved in? What opportunities for collaboration could you advance?

SuCCess

Solutions for Patient Safety team with 2018 John M. Eisenberg Patient Safety and Quality Award. Courtesy of Nick Lashutka, Ohio Children's Hospital Association.

As you reflect on these stories, jot down your own examples of successful collaboration and the people who are your collaboration role models.

Keys to Collaboration

- Network with others
- Share ideas
- Find common ground
- Celebrate together

Chapter 7
Communication

THE SPOKEN WORD IS a powerful force. It takes on special meaning when combined with positive values and actions, which always speak louder than words themselves.

People who are skilled communicators have influenced all of us. These individuals inspire others through their ability to listen, know their audience, connect in the moment and share their message. Communication between individuals is essential to developing trust, relationships, confidence and consensus.

Success depends on communication. People need to know their purpose and task, and they want to receive feedback.

We recognize effective communicators in our business and civic lives as well as in the realms of the media and performing arts; great communicators are all around us.

Communication is essential to finding success in all aspects of our life journeys. Communication in athletics is a key to successful teams. Communication in marriage and raising a family creates a trustworthy and nurturing environment. Communication in health care between providers and patients is an essential element of medical interventions.

We all know how confused and concerned we are when we are not part of a conversation and must rely on our own guesswork to understand what is happening. Communication in the workplace directly ties to morale, productivity, customer service, recruitment, retention and the ability to produce a successful product or service.

SUCCESS

Mean-spirited communication is also an unfortunate reality. It may produce a short-term gain or pad the ego of the person crafting the message, but people quickly assess the nature of the words and know when a message is self-centered, deceptive and divisive. This form of communication ultimately brings negative results.

We've all witnessed men and women who are gifted communicators. They have mastered the art of communication and know how to motivate and connect with their listeners, teams or organizations.

Communication is inspiring and creates an exciting, interactive culture.

I continue to learn from reading and listening to the words of gifted speakers and writers such as Rev. Martin Luther King Jr.; former presidents Franklin D. Roosevelt, John F. Kennedy and Ronald Reagan; and others including Rita Dove, Maya Angelou, Knute Rockne, Woody Hayes, John Wooden, Pat Summitt and many more persuasive people.

I've also been influenced by my coaches, teachers, parents, world leaders, elected officials, volunteers and children who simply know how to communicate well. In fact, it's often the communicators closest to home who have the most impact.

Several years ago during my time as CEO, Akron Children's invested in a major expansion of pediatric services in Youngstown, Ohio. We were invited into the Mahoning Valley region by another health care provider who knew we could significantly enhance access to pediatric services.

As plans were being prepared, we reached out to community members to hear their ideas and answer their questions. Early in the process, someone suggested I meet with Connie Knecht. Mrs. Knecht was a well-respected community member who was involved in numerous organizations and chaired countless initiatives.

I also found she was a wonderful storyteller and had a real-life story for every occasion. Connie was loved for her positive attitude, honest and candid feedback, and her ability to engage in conversation. Her community network was endless, and she was a go-to person in that area. She knew the pulse of the team, the needy, the city and more. Connie was a petite woman with an enormous presence. Her attire was always professional, and her smile captured everyone before the first hello.

I still recall my first meeting with her. She was welcoming, gracious, enthusiastic and very helpful. She wanted to hear our hospital's story, learn about our vision and offer her help. She obviously was a champion for children and had a sense of the needs we could meet. She knew how to build bridges between people and develop trusted relationships through honest, genuine communication.

Connie encouraged me to listen with my ears, eyes and heart. She assured me that once my heart understood her community, our message about investing in children would be one people would want to hear.

Through this heartfelt communication, the Akron Children's Hospital story began to unite people and explain the investment needed to reach our goal. As a result, the project was a success, and we are still improving health care for the children of that region.

Connie Knecht understood the formula for success: communicate in the right way for the right reason. And, heartfelt communication adds the right perspective to any message.

Connie passed away in 2017. Among the many tributes her family received was one from a family friend who wrote, "My parents affectionately referred to your mom as 'Mother Theresa' as she had such a big heart and was always looking out for everyone else!"

In December 2018 at the hospital's anniversary gala celebrating 10 years of service in the Mahoning Valley, Connie's son and his family's business provided a gift to all in attendance. The gift was an ornament in the form of a holiday star that was crafted by Wendell August Forge, a local metal ware company.

Connie truly was that star. She brought a twinkling light to her interactions, stories and everyday activities. We shared Connie's message at the gala, reminding everyone of her words of wisdom:

SuCCess

Listen not only with your ears but also with your eyes and heart so you can learn to communicate with others in a meaningful way.

When I talk about listening with your heart, my longtime friend Father Norman Douglas comes to mind.

I met Norm in college, and we became friends through our involvement at the Newman Center, a campus ministry. Norm entered the priesthood following college and has been a noted pastor at several churches.

Twenty years ago, he had an idea that took his ministry to a new level. Norm partnered with his friend, Larry Vuillemin, an Akron attorney and gifted arbitrator. Norm and Larry crafted an idea to improve the way people communicate with one another.

Accordingly, they formed a not-for-profit organization called Heart to Heart Communications. Norm was able to devote time to launch the initiative because the Catholic Diocese saw merit in the program and supported his efforts.

Connie Knecht and the holiday star ornament, given in her honor at the Akron Children's Hospital Mahoning Valley 10th anniversary gala in 2018. Courtesy of Knecht Family.

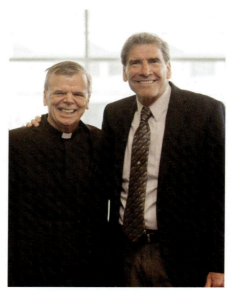

Good friends Father Norm Douglas (left) and Larry Vuillemin. Courtesy of Heart to Heart Communications.

Heart to Heart Communications is dedicated to the concept of listening with your heart and communicating with others from your heart. It's about breaking down barriers to communication and encouraging people to focus on what is really important in their lives.

Norm, Larry and their organization host an annual breakfast that attracts more than 1,000 people to hear the Heart to Heart message. The organization also works with local businesses to develop Heart to Heart support groups for segments of their workforces. The groups meet regularly with a facilitator to open communication channels and enable discussions about where participants are in their spiritual and well-being journeys.

Heart to Heart also sponsors monthly presentations where members of the community share their stories over breakfast. The initiative has become an important part of the fabric of our community.

SuCCess

Heart to Heart annual Greater Akron Speaks Out for Values breakfast. Courtesy of Heart to Heart Communications.

The organization is governed by a community board, which helps craft positive messages for problem solving through respectful, honest and heartfelt communication. People with differing views are brought to the table—a nonthreatening table, and one that is set for sharing ideas through discussion. Input from all individuals is welcome, and results and progress are regularly communicated.

Heart to Heart Communications groups function throughout our community. Their presence has enhanced our civic engagement, civility and awareness of others. What bubbles to the surface in these discussions is the realization of everything we have in common despite superficial differences that seem to divide us. This widespread communication has contributed significantly to Akron's success as an All-American City.

My daughter, Cathryn O'Malley, is a member of the Heart to Heart Communications board of directors and serves as the mistress of ceremony for the annual breakfast. She is convinced of the value of the Heart to Heart mission and believes, "the organization promotes open communication in a trusted, respected and safe environment."

Cathryn O'Malley speaking at the Heart to Heart breakfast. Courtesy of Heart to Heart Communications.

As in all meaningful communications, Heart to Heart brings authenticity, appreciation, awareness and a welcoming attitude to all interactions between people and organizations. The program brings out the best in people and is a key to their own success as well as to the success of all their other endeavors.

What forms of communication work best for you? What individuals have been role models as communicators? How has good communication assisted you in realizing success?

Keys to Communication

- Listen
- Show empathy
- Know your audience
- Speak from the heart
- Stay in the moment
- Make eye contact
- Provide feedback
- Be positive

Chapter 8
Commitment

AN ORGANIZATION THAT IS known for commitment to its mission, customers, workforce and ethical standards has the formula for success.

Committed people are true to their word. They embrace responsibility and are sought out for their leadership.

Commitment to a mission, marriage or set of beliefs and values provides strength when those values are threatened. People and organizations that uphold their commitments are widely trusted and can be a calming influence in times of uncertainty and challenge.

Commitment also promotes confidence when one must be an architect of positive change in uncertain times. Commitment does not mean maintaining the status quo. To the contrary, commitment promotes belief in the values and ethical behavior that are the key elements of an organization's success in advancing its mission in an honorable way.

True commitment must be to your underlying values, not to changing realities.

My parents are a wonderful example of commitment. They were married for 68 years, until my father died at the age of 93. As of this writing, my mom is still alive and keeping all of us committed to our family values and life's work.

Mom and Dad were fully committed and invested in their marriage vows and the responsibilities of parenting. They led by involvement and example, and were admired by their co-workers, friends, neighbors, children and other relatives.

Families often provide our first lesson in commitment.

The Magic of Michael Foundation is an inspirational story of one family's commitment in the face of adversity. The Hirschbeck family have shared their story and by doing so have touched countless lives while keeping alive the legacy of their two sons. Their commitment to one another is phenomenal and continues to this day.

John Hirschbeck was an elite Major League Baseball umpire for 32 years. He and his wife, Denise, had four children—John, Michael, Megan and Erin—and they led an all-star life.

They were a close-knit, committed family in spite of John's demanding career as one of baseball's best-known and popular umpires. John and Denise included their family on regular-season trips whenever possible, and they went to All-Star games and World

My parents, Gene and Howard. Courtesy of Considine Family.

SuCCess

Series championship games when he umpired. They handled their family's busy schedule until one day they were faced with a difficult challenge.

John and Denise's son, Michael, was born October 23, 1986, two years after the birth of his older brother, John, who was born October 9, 1984. At the ages of 5 and 7, both boys were diagnosed with adrenoleukodystrophy (ALD), a rare, genetic neurological disease that affects the white matter of the brain.

Michael was fortunate to receive a bone marrow transplant from his youngest sister, Megan. Sadly, John passed away at the young age of 8.

Michael, despite his many emergency room visits and hospital stays, never once complained or asked, "Why?" In fact, he always charmed his numerous doctors and nurses with his positive approach and spirit.

As his life progressed, Michael continued to spread his magic. He was extremely passionate about life, family, friends, money and baseball. His courage and tenacity were beyond reproach.

If you had the good fortune to know him, you were witness to the amazing character that was Michael Hirschbeck. His smile lit up his face and was reflected in his eyes. Unfortunately his life, which was much too short but full of so much, came to an unexpected end on April 8, 2014.

His family's commitment to each other continues to inspire others.

In memory of Michael and his brother, the Magic of Michael Foundation was born. Michael's magic lives on through the foundation's activities that support and enrich the lives of other families enduring challenging times or medical hardships.

Family friend Ed Muransky has seen their challenges over the years. "John and Denise have an amazing commitment to each other, their family and their community," he said. "They gave each other strength after agonizing over losing not one, but two of their children to a cruel disease. They were committed to giving their two

(From left) John and Denise Hirschbeck, Joe Torre (former manager and Baseball Hall of Famer), Erin Hirschbeck, Megan Hirschbeck. Courtesy of Hirschbeck Family.

daughters as much love and support as they could while they also mourned the loss of their brothers."

Ed noted that the Hirschbecks, "made it their mission to give back to the community they called home to help others going through similar difficulties. They are committed to ensuring that the lost lives of their sons will continue to make a difference in the lives of others."

Ed is a successful man himself. He grew up in Youngstown, Ohio, played football at Cardinal Mooney High School, and was recruited to play for The University of Michigan where he became an All-American. He played in the National Football League before

SuCCess

returning to the Youngstown area and developing a successful business portfolio.

For Ed, however, success is not just about a list of accomplishments. "One knows they are successful when there is a feeling of inner satisfaction at knowing you have performed to the peak of your ability," he said. "That nothing was held back in trying to achieve your goals, and that you can look in the mirror and know your accomplishments have come without compromising your moral and ethical beliefs."

That definition of success fits the character, courage, and commitment of the Hirschbeck family. John and Denise described that commitment as follows:

"As difficult as our lives have been since losing our two sons, we know that life goes on for our family. No day is ever the same, but through The Magic of Michael Foundation we have been fortunate to help other families in need."

Another individual who is a poster person for commitment, as well as other character traits in this book, is Patricia O'Desky.

When I was hired to be CEO of Akron Children's, the chairman of the board of directors gave me Pat's name as the person who could assist me if I had questions or needed information on the hospital regarding budgets, organizational charts, staff, objectives, etc.

I contacted Pat from my position at the hospital in Chapel Hill, North Carolina, prior to my transition, to request a number of documents and information on Akron Children's.

The next day, I received a packet from Akron that not only included answers to all my questions but contained very well-organized background information on the hospital with an executive summary. When I officially started at the hospital, Pat was temporarily assigned as my administrative assistant. Following a search process, I soon chose her as a permanent member of my team.

I found her commitment to the mission of the hospital and her standard of excellence were well-known throughout the entire

73

Bill Considine with his assistant of 40 years, Pat O'Desky. Courtesy of Akron Children's Hospital.

enterprise. Her work ethic was unsurpassed, and her skill set in dealing with people was admired by all.

Pat also embraced all the character traits important to success: respect, trustworthiness, responsibility, caring, fairness and more. As I write this book, Pat has now served Akron Children's Hospital for nearly 50 years, with 40 of those as my assistant.

Well before iPhones and iPads, I was fortunate to have an "iPat." Pat is more dependable than technology, and, as Mary Poppins would say, she's "supercalifragilisticexpialidocious."

Pat's commitment to excellence, to the hospital's mission and to a just and fair culture was recognized by her fellow employees in 2012 when they presented her with the coveted Distinguished Service Award. The award represents the hospital's highest honor and speaks to a person's commitment and respect as a role model for others.

SuCCess

In her acceptance speech, Pat shared the life journey that led her to Akron Children's. Pat, too, came from humble beginnings filled with her share of challenges. She attributes all the experiences she encountered in her life journey with making her the person she is today.

She recognizes the important role her mother played. Her mother set a high standard to make sure her five children grew up to be responsible adults who weren't afraid to work, who loved and cared for each other, and who always treated everyone with respect.

Although she didn't know it at the time, Pat's mother instilled in her children what is now referred to as having a "servant's heart." And servant leadership requires a high form of commitment.

My parents, the Hirschbeck family and my assistant, Pat O'Desky, are perfect examples of people who model commitment in all they do. Their involvement leads other people to find success and achievement in their own lives.

We need to love what we do! That type of commitment exudes from our words and actions. True commitment lets you speak from your heart. Belief in a mission helps people find the inner peace that allows them to deal objectively with tense, confrontational and stressful issues and schedules.

From the very beginning, countless members of our Akron Children's Hospital family have shown that commitment.

Commitment feeds our culture at Akron Children's. Commitment means being timely in following up on the promises we make or deadlines we need to meet. Commitment means being respectful of other people's time, thus being prompt for meetings. Commitment is about customer service, and being a continuous learner and a coach for others.

Commitment means fighting through mood swings and remaining positive. Commitment is never making your bad hair day someone else's. Commitment is being aware of your actions and cognizant of how they affect others. Commitment means going the extra mile. Commitment also means being willing to change what you do and not become trapped by a desire to maintain the status quo.

As leaders, we need to set the table for change and be the engine that empowers people to move forward. People who are civil, confident and consistent in their commitment command respect for their position and beliefs. Effective individuals know how to communicate their commitment and collaborate with those who hold other points of view.

This type of commitment leads to success.

Keys to Commitment

- Be responsible
- Be loyal to your mission and values
- Be dedicated to a standard of excellence
- Embrace actions over words

Chapter 9
Confidence

I GREW UP WITH MY friend, Peter Burg. Pete was born to a blue-collar family in East Akron. From early on, he was a confident young man. He attended Annunciation Grade School, St. Vincent High School (the future St. Vincent-St. Mary High School and alma mater of super-athlete LeBron James) and The University of Akron.

Following graduation, Pete went to work for the Ohio Edison Company, where his talents were quickly recognized. He held several leadership roles, and in 1999 was appointed president and CEO of FirstEnergy Corp., the company formed following a merger with Ohio Edison in 1997. It was a large leap for a hometown guy, and a monument to the value of his self-confidence.

Confidence is a crucial component of success. It is built over a lifetime through experiences, accomplishments and education—both formal and practical.

David James, superintendent of Akron Public Schools, has seen the importance of confidence in the countless number of students he has mentored over the years.

"To find one's passion, confidence is critical," James said. "It's that quality that gives us room to make mistakes—even to fail—while on a quest to stretch and try different things before we succeed."

We all know confidence when we see it. Confidence is projected through one's body language, spoken words, temperament, attitude and interactions with others. Personal success and organizational achievements are tied to confidence in a leader. People who believe in themselves and trust the abilities of others show confidence.

We have all seen athletic teams succeed in the face of phenomenal odds against them because they had confidence and believed in what they could achieve together.

Confidence generates the positive, can-do attitude that allows people to excel. Individuals know when they are in the presence of someone with confidence. Everyone is motivated and inspired by the spirit of confidence. They see how the improbable can become the probable. They also sense the belief these people have in others, generating their own confidence in themselves.

With confidence comes optimism, which assists in creating excitement around a vision for the future.

Arrogance, on the other hand, should never be confused with confidence. It is a sign of weakness, whereas confidence signifies strength.

But back to Pete Burg. Pete's confidence was evident throughout his life in his sports, academics and community involvements. Pete enjoyed competition and being part of a team. His confidence was on display in the sporting arena and later in his life in the corporate board room.

Pete's confidence gave him an inner peace as an athlete that created his positive mind-set and strengthened his belief in what was possible. His teammates thrived as a result of his confidence as a pitcher on the baseball mound, quarterback on the football team and point guard on the basketball team.

In all these roles, Pete was not the best athlete on the team. He was, however, the core of his team's confidence. He made all his teammates better competitors because they fed off of his confidence, win or lose.

In the business world, Pete was a confident, transformational leader because he could empower and excite his workforce. Pete never forgot his humble roots and identified with employees at

SUCCESS

all levels of his organization. He was comfortable and confident in who he was and exuded that inner peace.

His confidence also enabled Pete to engage with community leaders to develop collaborative plans that would address a variety of challenges facing his hometown. Pete brought people together and convinced the local chapter of our Red Cross they could raise the funds needed to build a new, expanded center.

Pete lent his talents to help solve numerous community issues. His involvement with regional chambers of commerce, not-for-profit organizations and local hospitals helped establish agendas that are still successfully addressing needs in his hometown communities.

Pete died in 2003, way too early. But his leadership spirit and lasting legacy are thriving because of the many lives he influenced over the years. His childhood sweetheart and wife of 36 years, Eileen, picked up the torch from Pete. She, too, believes in the

Eileen and Pete Burg. Courtesy of Burg Family.

power of people and is confident that when you invest in them, they will exceed your every expectation.

Pete and Eileen Burg were a caring, confident couple. They shared their love with family and friends, colleagues, community members and people in need. Their confidence allowed them to take chances, invest in people and believe in a bright future. They lit a beacon of light that continues to shine brightly in our community and serves as a signpost to success for those who share their values.

Fifty years after Pete Burg's graduation, another confident young man graduated from the same high school and excelled on the basketball court.

LeBron James played basketball at St. Vincent-St. Mary from 1999 to 2003. My youngest son competed against LeBron when they were in junior high school.

I witnessed LeBron's early years on the court and saw the confidence he had in his teammates and his enormous talent. He was also adept at making everyone on his team better at their positions because of his unselfish play, encouragement, example and constant effort.

His high school team went undefeated during his senior year and was rated No.1 in the country. That team was comprised of a group of young men from LeBron's neighborhood in Akron.

Following high school, LeBron entered the National Basketball Association, and the story of his success is well-known. He has won Olympic gold medals and NBA championships, including Cleveland's first championship in more than 60 years. He has been a league MVP, NBA All-Star and confident competitor.

Importantly, LeBron has remained connected to his hometown. In 2018 through his LeBron James Family Foundation and in partnership with Akron Public Schools, he launched the I PROMISE School, which enrolls young students at academic risk while they are still in elementary school.

The school requires students to sign an I PROMISE document. In it, students agree to meet the requirements of the rigorous

SuCCess

I PROMISE School in Akron. Courtesy of Ted Stevens.

academic curriculum, extended hours and a school year that runs longer than local public schools. There are also provisions for wraparound support services to help the students' families provide a stable learning experience at home.

The motto of the I PROMISE School says it all: "Nothing is given. Everything is earned."

When the promises are met, the students are also guaranteed a scholarship to The University of Akron.

Akron Public Schools Superintendent David James notes that the partnership has led the district to define new goals.

"LeBron James' support of the I PROMISE School has given us the confidence to . . . try something completely different, while giving us the space and the flexibility to correct our course and grow," he said.

One man familiar with the character of both Pete and LeBron is Keith Dambrot, former basketball coach at The University of Akron and now head coach at Duquesne University.

81

Dambrot was LeBron's high school coach for two years when St. Vincent-St. Mary's won their back-to-back state championships. He understands the importance of combining confidence with the ability to care about other people.

"These two men are confident yet compassionate and humble people," Dambrot told me. "Their successes are based on their ability to balance these three attributes."

Pete Burg and LeBron James are confident men who excelled in their chosen career paths. The confidence they showed in themselves and in their teams led to success in their lives, and they are continuing to bring about success in the lives of others.

How does confidence affect your life? What are your stories? How have you interacted with people who reject confidence and choose doubt and pessimism, which can doom projects and lives to failure from the outset?

Coach Keith Dambrot. Courtesy of Duquesne University.

Keys to Confidence

- Believe
- Prepare
- Be genuine
- Be a continuous learner
- Be thankful

Chapter 10
Courage

THE COWARDLY LION IN the movie *The Wizard of Oz* came to mind when I first started thinking about courage and how it is a key to success.

The lion was the king of the land, yet he didn't believe in himself until Dorothy and the Wizard convinced him otherwise. The lion already possessed courage; he simply needed confidence to project that belief in himself. The Wizard's solution was to give the lion a hero's medal, as a symbol for all to see.

Finding real courage is rarely that simple. We've all known or experienced the power of peer pressure or other influences. Following the crowd is tempting and may seem to be the easier choice. When faced with a tough decision, courage is required to make the right choice and do the right thing in the face of other pressures.

In his book, *Lives of Moral Leadership,* the Pulitzer Prize-winning author Robert Coles writes about true leaders who demonstrated courage in standing up to adversity. It was a key ingredient contributing to their credibility and moral authority. These leaders always had the courage to think of others even when they were under threat.

Moral leaders such as Mahatma Gandhi, Dr. Martin Luther King Jr., Robert Kennedy and Dorothy Day are profiled by Coles in powerful stories about their meaningful lives and the courage they exhibited in helping others.

Dorothy Day, a writer and advocate for the poor, spoke of the need for courage to come to the aid of the less fortunate: "Love casts

Success

out fear, but we have to get over the fear in order to get close enough to love them."

During my 40-year tenure as CEO of a children's hospital, I was inspired daily by the strength and courage displayed by our young patients and their families when facing challenging health care situations. In many instances, the children we treat become caregivers for their parents and siblings, in addition to the physicians, nurses and staff on their care teams.

Their attitudes and the courage they exhibit in the face of sometimes terminal diagnoses are truly remarkable. Children show no fear and project a bright future for others. The courage to face the unknown and at the same time think about how to bring out the best in others is a real gift.

In addition to the patients and families who helped me define true courage, I've also learned from others. Two of my models are Juvenile Court Judges William Kannel and Linda Teodosio.

Both share a philosophy of public service and commitment to child advocacy. They represent different generations, but their lives and careers display enormous similarities. They have shown true courage by giving their very best as elected public servants and advocates for children.

Judge Kannel, who passed away at age 83 in 2002, was a pioneer in establishing the juvenile court system in Summit County. His was the first such court in Ohio. He served as juvenile court judge from 1971 to 1989, and he was also a past president of the Ohio Association of Juvenile Court Judges.

Judge Teodosio, who later became a juvenile court judge, expressed her thoughts on holding the same post as Judge Kannel.

"The longer I am here, the more I respect him and his innovations," she said. "Until you walk in someone else's professional shoes, it's difficult to understand the challenges that come with the position."

Judge Kannel saw the need for a court focused on children and challenged traditional thinking within the justice system. He brought a transparent, understandable form of justice to the cases that came before his court. He was fair, consistent, caring and had the courage to make the right decisions for the right reasons, regardless of political or social pressures. He was always focused on promoting the best interests of the children before him and doing what was needed to help point them toward a brighter future.

He even suspended my driver's license for one month, despite our family friendship. Lesson learned.

Under his direction, the juvenile court won national acclaim for many innovative programs dealing with children, training advocates and promoting mutual cooperation with community organizations and resources.

In 1985, to celebrate the juvenile court building's 25th anniversary, Summit County Council renamed the building the William P. Kannel Juvenile Court Center to honor his years of service.

Judge Kannel served as an instructor in juvenile law at The University of Akron Law School and also taught courses in the Sociology and Law Enforcement departments.

"I will always remember that he told me to do what is best for the kids and everything else would take care of itself," Judge Teodosio said.

"I have carried that advice with me throughout my tenure," she said. "Whether I am making case or administrative decisions, I always go back to that question: Is what we are doing best for the kids?"

Judge Kannel was extremely active in his community, and he served many organizations in leadership roles and as a board member, including:

- United Way of Summit County
- The University of Akron Alumni Association
- Child Guidance and Family Solutions
- YMCA
- St. Vincent Church Council
- Kutz Foundation Charitable Trust Allocation Committee

- Nazareth Housing Foundation
- Shelter Care, Inc.

Throughout his career he received many awards, including the Bert A. Polsky Award from the Akron Community Foundation, St. Thomas Moore Award from the Akron Deanery and Akron Bar Association, Alumni Honor Award from The University of Akron, Outstanding Alumni Award from The University of Akron School of Law, Bishop Cosgrove Justice Award from the Catholic Commission of the Southern Region, YMCA Service to Youth Award, and induction into the Catholic Youth Organization Hall of Fame. He and his wife, Bea, received the United Way's Distinguished Service Award in 1974.

When Judge Kannel retired from the court, he became executive director of the Leadership Akron program, where he served for six years.

I came to admire Judge Kannel for his credibility, courage in reminding people of their responsibilities and for challenging a court system to better serve children and their families. He was a man of enormous moral leadership, and he was successful in his life's work because he possessed all the skills covered in each of this book's chapters.

A pivotal transformation for child justice came when Judge Kannel founded the Court Appointed Special Advocate/Guardian Ad Litem (CASA/GAL) program in Summit County.

CASA/GAL trains volunteers to represent the best interests of children in cases of child abuse and neglect. These dedicated volunteers advocate for vulnerable children who might not otherwise have a voice speaking for them in the courtroom.

The program has grown under Judge Teodosio and is now the largest such program in Ohio and the fourth largest in the nation. The personal attention and advocacy brought to their cases benefit the children in the system and the entire community by ensuring they are ultimately placed in safe, stable home environments.

Judge Teodosio, who was sworn in by Judge Kannel in 2002 less than a month before he passed away, now oversees the Summit County Juvenile Court. I know he would be proud of the court under her leadership.

She modestly credits another important legacy he left behind.

"Much of the staff I inherited upon taking the bench worked under Judge Kannel. They freely shared their wonderful ideas and demonstrated a willingness to change whatever was necessary to do what is best for kids," she said. "They taught me much of what I am sure they learned from Judge Kannel. What an honor it has been to serve with such a dedicated, compassionate crew."

Following her election in 2002, Judge Teodosio reestablished the credibility of the Kannel court. My hospital responsibilities provided the opportunity for me to see the workings of the court system and its connection to the community. Judge Teodosio showed courage when she addressed issues within the system and worked to fill gaps that occurred in the 14-year period following Judge Kannel's retirement.

Judge Teodosio campaigned on the message that she would do what's best for children, and she has lived up to her campaign promises. Like Judge Kannel, she is fair, caring, transparent and consistent in her rulings. She always places the best interest of each child first and foremost.

She has the courage to be a voice for children and ensures a culture of justice. She witnesses how too many of our children are being abused and neglected instead of being nurtured. She is required to make very difficult rulings on the cases before her, and she always has the courage to do what is right for the children.

Judge Teodosio and her family also had enormous courage in dealing publicly with a private tragedy, the accidental death of her 22-year-old daughter. Andrea Rose Teodosio was a remarkably talented young woman who lost her life in a skiing accident. Judge Teodosio and her husband ,Tom, are both public figures, and the news was on the front page. The family mourned and will never truly recover from the tragedy. They did, however, show courage in finding a way to celebrate her life and keep her generous spirit alive.

The family established the Andrea Rose Teodosio Foundation, which raises funds and supports numerous organizations dedicated to helping the elderly and underprivileged, as well as those that promote environmental, community and educational causes. The courage Linda and Tom shared with our community as a result of that tragic event is an example to all.

Singer-songwriter Elton John sings a song called "Candle in the Wind." Both Judge Kannel and Judge Teodosio have been candles burning brightly through wind and storms. In the song, Elton John sings that when the rains come, you do not know where to go.

In real life, both of these judges knew where to go—to a place that embraces courage and keeps the candle of justice burning brightly for all children.

"The lives of thousands of children have been positively impacted because of Judge Kannel's willingness to think outside the

Judge Linda Teodosio with her daughter Andrea Rose. Courtesy of Teodosio Family.

box, his faith in the people of Summit County and his commitment to do what's best for the kids," Judge Teodosio said.

The courage to make necessary changes becomes a way of life in well-led organizations. In Summit County, Judge Linda Teodosio is carrying on the legacy of her good friend and mentor, Judge William Kannel.

What examples of courage in the face of criticism have you seen? How has your personal courage led to a success that benefited others?

Keys to Courage

- Be true to your values and what's right
- Be yourself
- Persevere in the face of threats
- Be a champion to those in need
- Take responsibility

Chapter 11
Coaching

'VE ALWAYS FOUND THAT leadership and success have a close connection with coaching and coaches. Successful athletic teams, obviously, are comprised of talented men and women. But success comes only when a coach melds the varied individuals into a single unit.

The same can be said about workplace settings. True leaders are coaches who also realize they benefit from being coached. In my lifetime, I've had a variety of coaching experiences and witnessed several different approaches. At Akron Children's, we have made use of executive coaching sessions, and I've participated both as a learner and coach.

When we think of the word *coach*, we first think of athletics. We should also think about how we can adapt those coaching lessons from the world of sports to promote success in our organizations.

My wife, Becky, is an accomplished tennis player, and she's had a long-term passion for the sport. She was part of a women's tennis club in college in 1967 and was very involved in helping the team transition from club status to a varsity team. Recently, that college team won its conference championship, and my wife was thrilled to be part of the celebration.

Tennis has stayed relevant to Becky, largely because of the person who has been her coach for the last 40 years.

Barb Beattie is the consummate coach. She teaches values as well as tennis skills in her structured sessions. She is a gifted tennis player, and she's been able to bridge the player-to-teacher gap to assess an individual's talent and willingness to learn. She then communicates with her students in a nonthreatening, motivational manner.

Barb began her tennis journey as an early pioneer in women's tennis. She trained under Harry Hopman at his International Tennis Academy and played collegiate tennis at the University of South Florida.

Later, she played at the U.S. Open and toured on the Women's Tennis Association's Avon Futures and Virginia Slims circuits. She competed against some of the legends in women's tennis, gaining their respect and friendship.

Barb is a Certified Elite Tennis Professional of the U.S. Professional Tennis Association (USPTA). She is also certified by the USTA Junior Net Generation youth program. Her passion for tennis and desire to give back to the game led her to become a coach at an indoor facility in North Canton, Ohio, during the winter months, and she has served nearly 40 years as the tennis director at Portage Country Club in Akron.

She developed a reputation early on as the area's premier teacher and coach. She has taught many top-ranked junior players as well as top recreational junior and adult players. She enjoys observing their successes and is a wonderful role model in all aspects of tennis, as well as in life. She has become a tennis coach and a life coach through her actions and tennis clinics.

I'm a self-proclaimed spectator when it comes to tennis. I have watched the game played at all levels from beginner to junior to collegiate competitions and Wimbledon. I've watched Barb share her knowledge and enthusiasm for the game with players of all ages and skill levels.

As mentioned above, she is a life coach as well as a tennis coach while engaged with her pupils. I've always been impressed with the way she connects with junior players. Her sessions are skill-focused with a balance of fun and feedback. Her students are respectful and adhere to her disciplined approach. She creates a

SUCCESS

Tennis coach Barb Beattie. Courtesy of Beattie Family.

bond between teacher and student. Young players who advance their skills to compete at the high school and college levels keep Barb in the loop on their progress and often arrange a quick lesson during summer breaks.

"My purpose as a coach is to not only help my students become the best player but also to help prepare them to be the best person they can become," Barb said.

Through her coaching, Barb has enabled numerous people to be successful both on and off the court. She encourages participation in community projects, outreach and service above self.

Barb's talents and service have been recognized by her peers. She was inducted into the Stark County Amateur Sports Hall of Fame and was named a WHBC Stark County Sportswoman of the Year. She was also inducted into the YWCA Stark County Women's Hall of Fame as a community leader.

(From left) Tennis players Gay Cable, Becky Considine, coach Barb Beattie, Kathy Reed and Kim Bernlohr. Courtesy of Considine Family.

When Barb retired from coaching at Portage Country Club, the club sponsored a tribute dinner and designated that court No. 1 would be named in her honor.

Barb Beattie embraced the responsibilities of leadership, empowered people around her, mentored young professionals and shared her spirit through coaching. Her success has been defined through the achievements of others.

"My parents and coaches were my greatest gift and blessing to success, not only in tennis but in life," Barb said. "Their life lessons, guidance, love and support have carried with me throughout my professional career and personal life."

Personally, I've also benefitted from numerous coaches. A grade school football coach named Ray Kapper taught me confidence, hard work, sportsmanship and team work. Ray later became service director for the City of Akron and was a valued civic and community leader.

SuCCess

In high school, Coach Haines believed in preparation, communication, teamwork and sportsmanship on and off the basketball court.

In college, my soccer coach, Stu Parry, was adept at developing the entire individual. His connection to community, drive to compete at the highest level and philosophy of believing in yourself and your teammates exemplify a winning formula.

While in college, I met The University of Akron's football coach, a man who promoted the secret of success on and off the field through PMA, Positive Mental Attitude.

Coach Jim Dennison taught and lived that philosophy daily.

Even in retirement, he gets together with past members of his coaching staff and former players during the Christmas season for a lunch and storytelling session.

I attended one of those lunches in 2018 and was overwhelmed by the stories shared by the players and coaches about how the PMA philosophy assisted them, not just in sports but in

Coach Jim Dennison. Courtesy of Jim Dennison.

handling battles with cancer, family deaths, raising families and career successes.

Coach Dennison is obviously a successful coach, both on and off the field.

Jim Tressel, who coached The Ohio State University football team to a BCS national championship and is now president of Youngstown State University, shared his story of being a young assistant on Coach Dennison's football staff at The University of Akron.

When Tressel completed his college degree, he wanted to join a successful coach to learn more about the profession. He was presented with an opportunity at Penn State to work with Coach Joe Paterno. His other choice was a position with Coach Dennison at The University of Akron.

Obviously, the national standing of Penn State was very attractive, as was the chance to learn from Coach Paterno, but Coach

(From left) Jim and Ellen Tressel with Becky and Bill Considine. Courtesy of Considine Family.

Dennison also enjoyed enormous respect and achieved a high level of success with far fewer resources.

Tressel struggled with the decision and consulted his father, a well-respected coach at Baldwin Wallace University. Jim's father encouraged him to join Coach Dennison's staff.

Tressel never regretted the decision. During his stint there, Tressel learned from Coach Dennison about the philosophy of Positive Mental Attitude and saw it in action.

"I have often credited Coach D with the template for coaching success through attitude development and PMA," Tressel said.

Tressel achieved enormous success in coaching and life. He mentored countless young minds and passed on the power of PMA. Now, as president of Youngstown State, he keeps in touch with Jim, one of his most significant mentors.

Executive coaching in today's world has proven to be a valuable ingredient in sustaining success in leadership. Leaders who are open to evaluation, assessment and coaching keep their skill sets relevant.

Coaching aligns with the concept of being a continuous learner. It can assist in assuring you address problem areas in your own style.

Coaching helps leaders to be honest with themselves and better connected to their responsibilities and the expectations of their workforces. Coaching can also assist in honing a leader's mentoring skills and ability to coach others.

As Coach Dennison and Coach Tressel have demonstrated, a positive attitude is crucial to success in coaching and in life.

Keys to Coaching

- Be positive
- Be honest
- Be respectful
- Be a mentor and motivate others
- Be prepared

Chapter 12
Corporate Citizenship

A SOCIETY IS MEASURED BY how it treats its children, elderly and the disadvantaged. A community is measured, in part, by how its corporate entities invest their time, talent and resources.

The phrase "it takes a village to raise a child" also applies to corporate citizenship regarding companies and the communities in which they conduct business.

Corporate citizenship can take many forms and applies to not-for-profit organizations as well as for-profit entities, no matter their size. The willingness of corporations to be good citizens creates a sense of community that includes pride, purpose and civility.

When employees and associates of companies come together to create a humane bottom line and promote service above self, it generates enormous personal reward throughout the company and the community. Civic involvement of this nature can help to address a community's needs, lead to initiatives that generate momentum and growth, and promote hope for the future. Many of our nation's communities can share similar success stories.

The city of Akron is the community I know best. My wife, Becky, and I are native Akronites. Our roots in this community are deep, as our parents were born and raised here as well.

SuCCess

When we were growing up, Akron was known as the "Rubber Capital of the World" or the "Rubber City," and it was home to all the major American tire companies: The Goodyear Tire & Rubber Company, Firestone Tire & Rubber Company, B.F. Goodrich Company, General Tire Company, Mohawk Rubber Company, as well as their aerospace and defense-related divisions and other tire-affiliated companies.

Akron was also the home of the Quaker Oats Company, Roadway Trucking Company, Knight Newspaper organization, Ohio Edison and more. These companies and their executives, boards, management, retirees, employees and their families believed it was their responsibility to be involved in their communities as corporate citizens.

For example, my Cub Scout pack met in a B.F. Goodrich facility. Junior Achievement programs were sponsored by the tire companies. CEOs of these companies sat on the boards of hospitals, civic organizations and universities. They chaired United Way campaigns and supported school levies, the world-famous All-American Soap Box Derby, YMCA and Akron Urban League. Cultural and arts organizations also benefited from the leadership of these corporations, and their corporate workforces were given incentives to volunteer. Akron was and is an All-American City because of its engaged corporate citizens.

There has been enormous change in our city's corporate presence since my childhood, yet the mantle of corporate citizenship has been maintained, often by newer corporate citizens or long-standing corporate foundations.

The collaboration between businesses, government, not-for-profit organizations, charitable foundations, schools and religious organizations is inspiring. Here are a few examples I'd like to share.

WILLIAM H. CONSIDINE

MARKS FAMILY CORPORATE CITIZENSHIP BLUE LINE

Two neighborhood and high school friends, Harvey Nelson and Steve Marks, became business partners in 1987, starting a company known as Main Street Muffins in downtown Akron. They worked hard and built a national business, now known as Main Street Gourmet, that is still growing today.

The company has a workforce of 150 people who embrace corporate citizenship through their personal involvement in numerous community organizations. Approximately 20 years ago, Steve and his wife, Jeannine, decided to direct some of their financial success to a new Akron initiative, one that would involve the entire community.

Both Steve and Jeannine were avid runners and were familiar with marathons and their growing popularity. Their idea was to launch an Akron Marathon. They assembled interested individuals, enlisted corporate citizens and staged the first race in 2003.

Jeannine and Steve Marks. Courtesy of Bruce Ford.

Success

To assist the runners in staying on course, the city painted a Blue Line for the 26.2-mile route. The line begins at Stan Hywet Hall & Gardens, meanders through the city's neighborhoods and ends in the center of downtown at Canal Park, home stadium of our Cleveland Indian's affiliate baseball team, the Akron RubberDucks.

Over the years, the Blue Line has come to symbolize the community's pride and connectivity. "Run the Blue Line" is now a familiar phrase.

The race was a success from day one and, in 2015 it evolved into a race series comprised of an 8K/1-mile race in June, a half marathon/10K in August, and then the marquee event: the Akron Marathon, Half Marathon and Team Relay in September. Each race has a philanthropic aspect and is geared to all ages. The race attracts worldwide recognition and world-renown marathoners. In 2018, there were nearly 15,000 participants in the race series.

In 2015, Akron Children's Hospital and the Akron Marathon announced that the hospital stepped to the Blue Line to become the title beneficiary. Corporate and community partnerships forged by Akron Children's continued and grew the three-race series.

In addition, miracle patients from the hospital became Hero Patients. Our Hero Patients and corporate sponsors participate in Hero Zones at key mile markers along the race. These patient Hero Zones are very popular and tremendously inspirational for the runners in their race to the finish line. As runners follow the Blue Line, they get to see and experience one miracle story after another—along with cheers and high fives from the miracle children.

The Marks family's good corporate citizenship created the Akron Marathon, an event that generates enormous health benefits, community pride and engagement.

"Corporate citizenship is something that has been ingrained in our community and passed down from generation to generation," Steve Marks told me. "Corporate citizenship just makes good

Layla Popik, 2018 Akron Marathon Hero Patient, with Bill Considine. Courtesy of Akron Children's Hospital.

business sense. Owners and employees take pride in knowing their company is doing a lot more than is required."

Those words capture the formula for success.

GAR Foundation

As I stated earlier, Akron was home to Roadway Express, Inc. The ecosystem among the tire, trucking, auto part and rail industries created robust businesses in the area. Roadway Express was an example of a successful company led by strong believers in community involvement.

One of the founders, Galen Roush, decided to keep that spirit alive in his estate plan, creating what is now known as the GAR Foundation.

SuCCess

Historic GAR Foundation home. Courtesy of the GAR Foundation.

The GAR Foundation has been part of the community's fabric since 1967. Although Roadway Express no longer operates under that name, the community interest of the original company is alive and well.

The GAR Foundation's current president, Christine Amer Mayer, a native Akronite herself, is committed to the meaningful work of GAR.

"The mission of GAR Foundation is to help Akron become smarter, stronger and more vibrant," she said. "This mission points to our strategic work in education, economic development and the arts, all of which were causes that Galen and Ruth Roush supported in their lifetimes.

"The Roush family built their company on core values of hard work, integrity, honesty and humility. When that recipe served them well, creating a company that was a national leader, they never forgot the community that supported them from their humble beginnings. They established GAR Foundation, thereby enabling perpetual reinvestment in the community they loved," Mayer said.

103

GAR has created impact through its grants and by encouraging community collaboration. In fact, today the GAR Foundation awards $6 million annually to organizations and programs related to education, the arts, workforce and economic development and others. One specific community not-for-profit initiative which GAR has supported is the Summit Education Initiative (SEI). SEI has developed a process in which educators can use data and predictive analytics to understand how to improve the educational experience of their students.

GAR is a great example of how corporate citizenship can have a lasting legacy long after the company and its workers have moved on.

Goodyear Tire & Rubber Company

The Goodyear "Wingfoot" magic continues to enrich the Akron community. As I mentioned, the Goodyear presence was a constant

Wingfoot One flies over The Goodyear Tire & Rubber Company's airship hangar at Wingfoot Lake in Suffield, Ohio. Courtesy of The Goodyear Tire & Rubber Company.

during my childhood. For the last 40 years, that presence has continued even though the business has changed. Tires, with the exception of race tires, are no longer made in Akron, yet the global corporate headquarters remains here. Goodyear is still a major employer although with far fewer employees than during the peak tire-production years in Akron.

In my past capacity as CEO of Akron Children's, I can attest to Goodyear's belief in corporate citizenship. The company has been generous to the hospital over the years. Its executives have served on our board of directors, and we have partnered on numerous community events and initiatives.

One of those partnerships is known as the Safe Mobility Project. The focus of the Safe Mobility Project is to reduce the danger to children in Summit County from accidental injuries as they move around our communities.

The Goodyear Foundation partnered with Akron Children's to create a group of programs targeted at improving the health and well-being of children ages birth through 18 that address child passenger safety, pedestrian safety, wheeled sports safety and teen driving safety.

Through the Goodyear Foundation's support of this project during Phase 1, Akron Children's has provided families with 3,426 car seats, 4,242 bike helmets and various forms of education regarding teen-driving safety. So far in Phase 2 covering the period of January to June 2019, we have distributed an additional 178 car seats and 359 helmets.

In 2017, the safemobilityproject.com website launched with a car seat selector, educational videos, helmet-fit test, teen safe-driving pledges and much more.

Since its inception in March 2016 through June 2019, the Safe Mobility Project has conducted or participated in more than 229 events with 302 volunteer opportunities and engaged 112 Goodyear associates with the program. The Goodyear Foundation's financial commitment began with a grant in 2016 and continues today.

Goodyear also partners with the Akron Children's Hospital Akron Marathon Race Series to promote and sponsor a half marathon and 10K as part of a three-race series. The half marathon starts on the famed Goodyear test track and proceeds through the East Akron community that is home to Goodyear's corporate headquarters.

These are just two examples of Goodyear's current engagement with the community. Its CEO, Richard J. Kramer, is continuing the corporate citizenship legacy of his predecessors in many more ways.

"At Goodyear," he said, "we are firm believers in giving back to the communities where we operate, to help them be safe, smart and sustainable. Over my long friendship with Bill Considine, I have seen time and time again that this is core to who he is as well. Corporate citizenship is as much his identity as his role as the longtime leader of a major Akron institution."

Ohio Edison/FirstEnergy Corporation

Another model corporate citizen is FirstEnergy, which sets a high bar for other local companies.

Reddy Kilowatt sign. Courtesy of Considine Family.

SuCCess

My father worked at Ohio Edison, and growing up we were all "Reddy Kilowatt" fans.

Ohio Edison touched many lives through its support for our not-for-profit community organizations. Today, FirstEnergy's top management takes important leadership roles within Akron and supports companywide involvement as well. The company's community presence is extensive. Here are a few examples:

Akron has been home to the iconic All-American Soap Box Derby since 1934. The Derby brings together young people from around the world to compete in gravity-powered racers. When the Derby lost its primary sponsor several years ago, FirstEnergy came to the rescue. The Derby today is thriving because of FirstEnergy's involvement and belief in the children who travel from around the world to participate.

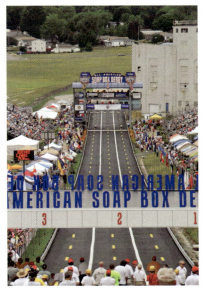

Derby Downs in Akron, home of the All-American Soap Box Derby. Courtesy of Mark Gerberich, International Soap Box Derby, Inc.

107

William H. Considine

Last year, 433 boys and girls aged 7 to 20 years created lifelong memories and friendships on the Derby Downs track. The success of the Derby and the community's engagement led actor and director Corbin Bernsen to produce the movie *25 Hill* in 2011.

FirstEnergy has also invested in downtown Akron development and our public schools, and partners with Akron Children's Hospital and the Akron Marathon in staging the Akron Children's Hospital Akron Marathon Race Series Marathon, Half Marathon & Team Relay. In 2018, the Marathon in September attracted nearly 9,000 runners and featured 18 Hero Patients from the hospital. The highlight of the evening before the race is a child/family run through downtown that attracts nearly 1,000 additional participants.

FirstEnergy also sets the standard of support for our food bank, United Way, Heart to Heart Communications and more.

(From left) Akron Children's Hospital Chairman of the Board John Orr, Akron Children's CEO Emeritus Bill Considine, First Energy President and CEO Chuck Jones and his grandchildren. Courtesy of Jones Family.

SuCCess

FirstEnergy's corporate support in all of these endeavors promotes health, teamwork and community pride. Its executives are admired for their services to community.

Charles E. Jones, president and CEO of FirstEnergy, has a long personal connection to Akron.

"As a native Akronite who grew up near FirstEnergy's downtown headquarters, some of the most rewarding experiences of my career have been those opportunities to get involved and make our community a better place to live and work," he said. "When I talk with leaders at FirstEnergy, I stress that our commitment to corporate citizenship stems from our belief that our company is only as strong as the communities we serve."

As if to reinforce the message of this book, Jones tells his executive team that "as leaders 'SuCCCCes' is spelled with 4 Cs: consistency, caring, communication and courage."

Akron Paint & Varnish

The south side of Akron, sometimes known as L.A., for Lower Akron, was the home of the Firestone Tire & Rubber Company. When the company became Bridgestone Corporation, and its consumer tires were no longer made in Akron, the neighborhood changed. One company that remained in the area was Akron Paint & Varnish, Inc. The business is owned by the Venarge family—Dave and his wife, Cheryl, and his son, Tom, and his wife, Marcy.

Dave is a native of Akron and has deep roots in South Akron. For those of you who may remember the South Akron Rangers football team, Dave was a member of the Ranger's championship team.

Dave and his family, along with his business team, have developed a flourishing enterprise with worldwide clients. Their global success has not diminished the Venarge family's commitment to their neighborhood.

When a cemetery near his business was in disrepair, Dave stepped forward to upgrade and maintain the grounds, restoring

Dave Venarge with development plans. Courtesy of Mike Cardew, *Akron Beacon Journal.*

dignity to the grave sites. He's now working with Summit County and other partners to develop a business and office park on property that was left vacant after the Bridgestone-Firestone headquarters relocation. His investments of time, talent and financial resources are revitalizing a legendary and proud South Akron neighborhood.

In addition, Dave's generosity benefits numerous not-for-profit organizations through contributions of time and funds he and his family have established through the Akron Community Foundation.

Dave and his family are champions for our community and valued corporate citizens.

LEAFFILTER GUTTER PROTECTION

In 2005, Matt Kaulig started LeafFilter in the basement of the home he shares with his wife, Lisa. Today, Matt has positioned LeafFilter as a leader in rain gutter protection across the country.

SuCCess

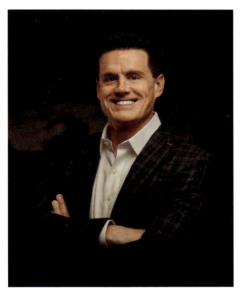

Matt Kaulig. Courtesy of Justin Domhoff, Kaulig Media

Significant business achievements aside, Matt and Lisa believe that with success comes the responsibility to give back to the community.

Matt and Lisa are both graduates of The University of Akron. Matt, a former quarterback for The University of Akron's Zips football team, continues to lead his alma mater as an alumnus. He is a strong promoter of the university's academic programs and colleges. And he makes it fun—appearing in commercials and podcasts with a variety of props aimed at building awareness and recruiting students.

Akron Children's Hospital is near and dear to Matt and Lisa. One day after their daughter was born, she required surgery and spent time in our Neonatal Intensive Care Unit (NICU). Perhaps this is why Matt's business model centers in part on the healing power of giving back.

This approach led him to get involved in a program called "Santa PICsU" that supports the patients in the hospital's Pediatric Intensive Care Unit (PICU)." Matt and a team of other elves hold events that raise funds to ensure year-round Christmas gifts for children in the hospital's PICU, especially during the holidays. Santa PICsU also generated funds to purchase new waiting room furniture and hospital equipment.

Matt continues to promote the healing power of giving through the Matt and Lisa Kaulig Family Foundation and Kaulig Giving. He and Lisa retain a special interest in the NICU at Akron Children's. Most recently they held a golf experience that raised money for special ventilators to help the tiniest of babies in our NICU.

Matt's company is realizing enormous growth and success because he embraces the characteristics described in this book. Matt Kaulig exemplifies corporate citizenship.

KEN BABBY, AKRON RUBBERDUCKS

In 2012 at the age of 32, Ken Babby acquired the Akron Aeros, a Double-A minor league baseball team affiliated with the Cleveland Indians. In 2014, after fan-involved surveys and contests to pick a new name, the team became the Akron RubberDucks, a whimsical name that connects back to Akron's rubber history.

Babby reduced ticket prices, renovated the stadium with private funds and revamped the concession stands with the goal of providing a family-friendly environment. Ken embraced corporate citizenship, community, collaboration and children with genuine dedication and passion. He understands family and is committed to providing a wholesome fan experience.

The popular venue and modernized stadium also provide a valuable entertainment anchor to the southern end of downtown Akron.

Ken Babby understands partnerships and works with numerous groups to promote their success. Through corporate citizenship, he gives his time, talent and funds to advance the entire community.

SuCCess

2018 Cancer Survivors' Night at Akron RubberDucks stadium. Courtesy of Akron Children's Hospital.

He's personally involved in health care organizations, United Way, scouting, local schools and the Downtown Akron Partnership.

His general manager, Jim Pfander, has a daughter who was diagnosed and treated for a childhood cancer. Her cancer is in remission, yet Ken Babby's advocacy for children dealing with cancer is truly amazing.

Each year Ken partners with Akron Children's Hospital to host a cancer survivor night. Patients design the team's game uniform, the players each team up with a child, and prior to the first pitch thousands of families surround the field and release balloons. Ken and his caring organization supported the Pfander family and continue to support countless other families.

As a successful businessperson, Ken has received several awards for excellence. Yet his real key to success is his belief in people and community, and his love of family. His wife, Liz, and son, Josh, complete his all-star team.

WILLIAM H. CONSIDINE

THEKEN FAMILY OF COMPANIES & NEXTSTEP COMPANIES

For my friend Randy Theken, who grew up in Barberton, Ohio, corporate success began at our alma mater, The University of Akron.

As a graduate student, Randy had the opportunity to obtain an undergraduate degree in electrical engineering and went on to obtain a master's degree in biomedical engineering under his mentor Dr. Glen O. Njus, who inspired his entrepreneurial spirit.

Between his studies, working for Dr. Njus and living in a broom closet in the Sidney L. Olson Research Center so he could keep a close eye on his research projects, Randy launched the first of his many businesses, Theken Orthopaedic, on his property in Coventry Township. Theken Orthopaedic provided mechanical testing and FDA regulatory and product development services to medical device companies for orthopedic implants.

From this humble start, Randy's influence on the spinal implant industry was unparalleled for more than 20 years. He founded several medical device companies in addition to Theken Orthopaedic, including Theken Spine (1998), Theken Disc (2003) and Therics (2005).

In 2009, Integra Life Science came calling and purchased three of these medical device companies for $200 million. Randy served as president of a new division within Integra Life Science called Integra Spine for nearly two years. What followed next for Randy, after his five-year noncompete, was the NextStep Companies. Currently he is creating, building and growing several new medical device companies, including NextStep Arthropedix, NextStep Extremeties and Theken Ceramics.

Randy's success allowed him to locate his businesses anywhere in the country, but he chose Akron as the place to invest his talents. His businesses are headquartered in Akron's original airport terminal building located on the southeast side of Akron near the former Goodyear Airdock, All-American Soap Box Derby hill, Rubber Bowl football stadium and the original Strickland's Frozen Custard stand. I have many wonderful memories of visiting and attending

SuCCess

events at all of these landmarks, but in recent years, the neighborhood has been in decline.

Randy's commitment to rebuilding and reinventing this part of Akron is a tremendous example of good corporate citizenship. Not only did he transform the historic Akron Fulton Airport Terminal building into his headquarters, he recently completed building a new $16 million manufacturing facility that will bring new skilled jobs to Akron.

Randy also gives back to his community through his time and philanthropy. He's helped our local schools build playgrounds, supported families in crisis and assisted Akron Children's Hospital in realizing its promise of ensuring that every child, no matter their circumstances, has access to high-quality health care.

Timken Foundation

There is one other corporate citizen that should be mentioned. The Timken Foundation of Canton has been an important partner for Akron Children's and has provided long-standing support to many regional organizations.

The Timken Foundation was created in 1934 by Henry H. Timken Sr. and his sisters, Amelia Bridges and Cora Burnett. The Timken family, through the foundation, has distributed more than $350 million in grants, mostly to communities where Timken and TimkenSteel operate.

In 2018, the Timken Foundation gave $1.5 million to support the new Akron Children's Health Center in North Canton, extending pediatric primary care, specialty care and rehabilitation services. Timken Foundation funding specifically goes toward pediatric medical equipment, security systems, information technology and furnishings for exam rooms and waiting areas. This support allows Akron Children's to partner with not only the Timken Foundation but also with Aultman Hospital and the A. Altman Company—all to benefit the health of the area's children.

William H. Considine

The Timken Foundation Building at Akron Children's Health Center opened in North Canton in May 2019. Courtesy of Akron Children's Hospital.

There are numerous other examples of corporate citizenship that could be highlighted. These companies involve their people and create a wonderful culture. In today's world, some companies have boards or executives who only measure success by their short-term bottom line and stock price. This is unfortunate, and often the communities and individuals who have sacrificed through tax breaks and other incentives to assist those companies are forgotten and marginalized.

What examples of corporate citizenship have you witnessed? What ideas for corporate citizenship would make sense for your employer or a not-for-profit you know?

Keys to Corporate Citizenship

- Executive involvement on community boards
- Empower your workforce to be involved in the community
- Mentorship programs
- Collaboration

Afterword
Children

WHEN PLANNING THIS BOOK on the attributes of success as defined by words beginning with the letter C, I thought I should start with what is, for me, the ultimate word: CHILDREN.

If our children aren't successful, we can't claim success for ourselves, either as individuals or a society. As adults, are we living up to our responsibility to nurture the promise of the next generation and ensure they have the chance for a bright future? Think of the costs if we fail.

We should all keep alive the spirit of a child, their innocence, honesty and sense of wonder. The beauty of a child's outlook is refreshing, and we need to be reminded as we grow older to see the world from their point of view.

I have learned to design a hospital facility through the eyes of a child and bring that perspective into my daily interactions. I've also asked myself routinely, what does a child see in what we do?

The book *Leadership* that I authored in 2017 was inspired by children who were cared for at Akron Children's Hospital. Their stories serve as life lessons, illustrating important traits of leadership. The stories are also wonderful examples of success.

Here are a few of those stories:

I recall meeting the family of Lucas Rife when they were dealing with a cancer diagnosis after doctors found a tumor in his leg bone. The family was very supportive of Lucas, and he was a positive influence on his family and his entire care team.

Lucas always had a good word for everyone and was determined to beat his disease. He became one of the hospital's miracle kids and was an inspiring spokesperson and role model. In public appearances, Lucas was asked what he wanted to do as an adult, and he immediately responded: "Succeed Mr. C. and be president of Akron Children's!" No doubt he could have easily embraced that role.

Lucas has thrived in spite of having his leg amputated. He is now in early adulthood, married to a wonderful young woman and has a career as an ordained minister.

His determination and dedication helped him realize his dream of touching other people's lives through his work. All leaders should be as dedicated as Lucas in following their dreams.

Lucas Rife and his family. Courtesy of Akron Children's Hospital.

SuCCess

Lucas and Amanda Rife. Courtesy of Rife Family.

I met another young man, Trevor Weigand, during his multiple hospital stays for cancer treatment, including 12 surgeries. Trevor became a caregiver in his own style and empowered numerous people to fight both the ravages of cancer and fear of their cancer diagnosis.

Trevor received a blimp ride in recognition of his courageous battle with cancer, and he and his family had a wonderful experience. In fact, it was so enjoyable Trevor wanted other cancer patients he knew to enjoy the same experience. He championed the idea, talked to influential people and was able to arrange a ride for a group of patients through the Goodyear Tire & Rubber Co. He empowered others to use their resources to help his fellow patients.

But Trevor wasn't finished. His family is also very involved in basketball. His dad is a college coach, and his brother played on his high school team. Using these connections, Trevor reached out to a group of students who formed a network among several schools.

The high school students held meetings to discuss how they could promote cancer awareness. They launched a fundraiser called "Trevor's Team" that schedules events on Friday nights during the high school basketball season. Five games involving 10 teams are played with half of the gate receipts designated to the Trevor Fund for cancer awareness. One of the game sites also stages a chili cook-off to engage even more supporters.

By openly sharing his story and being a role model, Trevor empowered many people to use their imagination and skills to raise funds that touch countless lives.

As we prepare for the future, we as a society need to learn from Lucas, Trevor and our other miracle children about the importance of being more child-focused.

Trevor Weigand and his parents Jodi and Terry with NBA player Kosta Koufos. Courtesy of Weigand Family.

SuCCess

In this country, we routinely hear that children are our future. Recent studies have shown, however, that our nation's children are a forgotten group when it comes to investing in their health care and educational needs.

If we are going to sustain our economy and global standing as a productive, thriving nation, we must invest in our children's health and lifelong learning. As our society ages and a rapidly increasing number of adults retire from the workforce, we must ensure there is a viable base of young workers ready to take their place.

We need an identifiable children's health care program that is accessible, predictable and uniform from state to state to ensure that all children in our country have the chance to grow and reach their full potential as productive adults. Our educational system also needs to be structured to teach all children regardless of their economic status, ZIP code, race or gender.

It's worth noting that Medicaid is the No. 1 provider of coverage for children in this country, yet Medicaid is not recognized as a children's brand. As it's now structured, Medicaid provides medical care to our country's most vulnerable children. However, it also covers nursing homes and provides coverage through the Affordable Care Act to adults aged 26 to 64. In fact, half of our nation's children rely on Medicaid. Of the 74 million children in the United States, 37 million are covered by Medicaid, with an additional 1 million in Affordable Care Act Marketplace plans.

Medicaid is also critical to families of those who serve in the nation's armed forces. An estimated 3.6 million children of military families receive health coverage from Medicaid, including 3.4 million children of veterans.

Yet the Medicaid program is fragmented when it comes to serving children. We can do better. Although children account for 51 percent of all enrollees, they represent just 19 percent of Medicaid spending.

Studies show that children enrolled in Medicaid do better in school and have fewer sick days. They are more likely to graduate from high school and attend college. They grow up to be healthier adults and, as a result, will earn higher wages and pay more taxes. That means they will enjoy a higher standard of living and improve the quality of life in their communities.

The importance of enhancing access to child health care is evident when you consider that the health profile of children today is deteriorating. We continue to make astounding advances in pediatric medicine, yet barriers to care remain. And young people growing up in our society across all income levels face increased pressures from a variety of factors. Access to care continues to be a primary concern. Poverty plagues both urban and rural communities, resulting in families who lack access to healthy diets, affordable housing and safe neighborhoods.

Obesity and chronic diseases such as asthma and diabetes are on the rise. Our infant mortality rate continues to lag far behind most developed nations. Behavioral health issues involving suicide, substance abuse and exposure to violence have all increased dramatically among our youth.

We must craft a success formula for our children and put it in place. We need to develop an identifiable nationwide health program just for children. The Children's Health Insurance Program (CHIP) could be that program, but it needs to be adequately funded.

If children are the future as we claim, a comprehensive children's strategy should be developed that prioritizes our nation's children.

What are your ideas for putting together a success formula for children? How should we define success for our nation's 74 million children?

Our future depends on our investments in our children. Let's make 2020 and the decade that follows the Time for the Child!

Keys to Children

- Identify their needs
- Invest in their future

Acknowledgments

ANY PROCEEDS DERIVED FROM this book and my previous book, *Leadership,* are earmarked for the Rebecca D. Considine Research Institute and the advocacy efforts of Akron Children's Hospital.

A group of true champions for children assisted in this book's development and publication.

Pat O'Desky, who is mentioned in the chapter on commitment, was a sounding board and typist, preparing numerous drafts. Bernett L. Williams, Beth Smith, Anne Merchant, Karen Adams, Charlie Solley, Ted Stevens and Nick Lashutka all assisted by reading various drafts and being fact-checkers.

Ron Kirksey lent his enormous journalism skills to the writing and offered substantial suggestions for the final copy. Ron's assistance, with his extensive experience as a former journalist and communications consultant, proved invaluable.

My wife, Becky, was a source of encouragement and showed enormous patience relative to my regular musings.

The individuals, both adults and children, mentioned throughout the book were a constant inspiration and source of strength that kept me focused.

I want to thank everyone who contributed their stories and the personal comments that were included.

It is an honor and a humbling experience to share these stories and my perspective on success. I hope you enjoyed reading the book and will share your success with others.

About the Author

Bill Considine in Italy, 2019. Courtesy of Considine Family.

Bill Considine was born in Akron, Ohio, in 1947 to Howard and Gene Marie Considine. The oldest of five children, he has one sister and three brothers. He married Rebecca D. Krenrick in 1972, and they have three children, Michael, Cathryn (married to Michael O'Malley) and Matthew (married to Becca Mayors), and two grandchildren (twins Jemma and Graeme).

Bill served the United States as a Lieutenant in the Public Health Service during the Vietnam conflict and received an honorable discharge.

William H. Considine

While in college at The University of Akron, Bill lettered on the soccer team and was student government president in 1969. He was in the first master's degree program class for Hospital and Health Service Administration at The Ohio State University and has been recognized with its Distinguished Alumni Award.

He worked at North Carolina Memorial Hospital from 1972 to 1979 before being appointed president and CEO at Akron Children's Hospital in 1979.

Bill served as board chairman of the National Association of Children's Hospitals and Related Institutions from 1988 to 1990, board chairman of the Child Health Corporation of America from 1990 to 1992 and board chair of the Children's Miracle Network from 1996 to 1998. He was honored with the Network's Founders Award in 2019.

Bill has honorary doctorates from The University of Akron and Northeast Ohio Medical University. He served on numerous

Bill and Becky Considine. Courtesy of Considine Family.

SuCCess

boards and has been recognized, with his wife, for philanthropic generosity. He is a fellow in the American College of Healthcare Executives and is an active, popular speaker and advocate for children's health care investment.

In 2009, Bill was inducted into the Northeast Ohio Business Hall of Fame. He is a member of the Ohio Business Roundtable and was appointed to the board of the John S. and James L. Knight Foundation in 2011. He continues to serve on the boards of numerous Akron-area community organizations and has been honored by many of these organizations. In 2006, the American Red Cross honored him with the H. Peter Burg Community Leadership Award. In 2011, the Akron Community Foundation presented him with the Bert A. Polsky Humanitarian Award in recognition of his many years of community service.

During Bill's tenure at Akron Children's Hospital, the hospital thrived and grew in its mission of advancing family-centered care. The initial hospital infrastructure he embraced in 1979 included approximately 1,200 employees and a $35 million budget. Today, the hospital enterprise employs more than 6,300 people with a $1 billion operating budget.

References

Angelou, Maya. Quotes. (n.d.). *BrainyQuote.com*. Retrieved June 28, 2019, from https://www.brainyquote.com/quotes/maya_angelou_392897.

Character. 2019. In *Merriam-Webster.com*. Retrieved June 28, 2019, from https://www.merriam-webster.com/dictionary/character.

Civility. 2019. In *Merriam-Webster.com*. Retrieved June 28, 2019, from https://www.merriam-webster.com/dictionary/civility.

Coles, Robert. (2000). *Lives of Moral Leadership.* New York, NY. Random House Trade Paperbacks.

Day, Dorothy. (January 1967). In Peace Is My Bitterness Most Bitter. *The Catholic Worker Movement.* Retrieved June 29, 2019, from https://www.catholicworker.org/dorothyday/articles/250.html.

Elton John and Bernie Taupin. (1973). "Candle in the Wind." *Goodbye Yellow Brick Road.* MCA Records.

Goman, Carol Kinsey. (Feb. 13, 2014). 8 Tips for Collaborative Leadership. *Forbes.* Retrieved June 29, 2019, from https://www.forbes.com/sites/carolkinseygoman/2014/02/13/8-tips-for-collaborative-leadership/#3865d535fd98.

Krzyzewski, Mike with Donald T. Phillips. (2000). *Leading with the Heart: Coach K's Successful Strategies for Basketball, Business, and Life.* New York, NY. Warner Books, Inc.

McKee, Robert. (June 23, 2015). *Is it Possible to Bring Storytelling into Marketing?* Retrieved June 29, 2019, from https://mckeestory.com/is-it-possible-to-bring-storytelling-into-marketing.

Pike, Albert. Quotes. (n.d.). *BrainyQuote.com*. Retrieved June 28, 2019, from https://www.brainyquote.com/quotes/albert_pike_101379.

Sheridan, Bill. (December 8, 2016). *Let's Redefine What 'Success' Means.* Retrieved June 28, 2019, from https://blionline.org/2016/12/lets-redefine-success-means.

Index

Italic page numbers indicate photos

A
A. Altman Company, 115
Affordable Care Act, 121
Akron Children's Hospital, *ix, x*
    founding/history, v–x, *vii, viii,*
        15, 50
    polio treatment, 14–15, *14*
Akron Marathon/Akron Children's
    Hospital Akron Marathon
    Race Series, 100–101, 108
    Blue Line, 100–102
    corporate sponsorship, 106, 108
    Hero Patients/Hero Zones,
        101, *102*
Akron Metropolitan Housing
    Authority (AMHA), 40–41
Akron Paint & Varnish,
    109–110
Akron RubberDucks, 112–113, *113*
Akron Symphony, 46
Akron: City at the Summit
    (Knepper), 49
All-American Soap Box Derby,
    107–108, *107*
AMHA (Akron Metropolitan
    Housing Authority), 40–41
Anderson, Jim, 58
Andrea Rose Teodosio
    Foundation, 89

Angelou, Maya, 20
Aultman Hospital, 115

B
Babby, Josh, 113
Babby, Ken, 112–113
Babby, Liz, 113
Beattie, Barb, 91–93, *93, 94*
Bernlohr, Kim, *94*
Bernsen, Corbin, 108
Bert A. Polsky Humanitarian
    Award, 10, 42, 45,
        87, 127
Blue Line (Akron Marathon),
    100–102
Bridges, Amelia, 115
Bunts, Helen, 27–28, *27*
Burg, Eileen, 32, 79–80, *79*
Burg, Peter, 9, 77–80, *79*
Burnett, Cora, 115

C
Cable, Gay, *94*
caring, 26–33
    Bunts, Helen, 27–28, *27*
    Cassidy (Jackson), 30–32, *31*
    Friebert, Dr. Sarah, 26,
        28–33, *29*
    keys to, 33

"Palette of Care" painting by
   Cassidy Jackson, 31–32, *31*
   palliative care, 28–32
CASA/GAL (Court Appointed
   Special Advocate/Guardian
   Ad Litem), 87
Cassidy (Jackson), 30–32, *31*
character, 5–11
   definition, 7
   keys to, 11
   Maynard, Philip H., 5–11, *11*
Character Counts! program, 6, 22
children, 117–122
   Cassidy (Jackson), 30–32, *31*
   courage, 85
   Hero Patients, 101, *102*
   keys to, 122
   Layla (Popik), Hero Patient, 102
   Lucas (Rife), 117–118, *118, 119*
   Trevor (Weigand), 119–120
Children's Health Insurance
   Program (CHIP), 122
civility, 19–25
   definition, 19
   keys to, 25
   respect, 20
   Rev. Dr. Ronald Fowler, 20–25,
      21, 24
   Rev. Knute Larson, 24–25, *24*
Clark, Mark and Cathy, 32
coaching, 91–97
   Beattie, Barb, 91–93, *93, 94*
   Dambrot, Keith, 81–82, *82*
   Dennison, Jim, 95–97, *95*
   Kapper, Ray, 94–95
   keys to, 97
   Krzyzewski, Mike, 51
   Parry, Stu, 95
   Tressel, Jim, 96–97, *96*

Coles, Robert, 84
collaboration, 50–61
   Father Richard (Rick) Frechette,
      55–58, *56*
   Goman, Carol Kinsey,
      50–51
   high reliability organizations
      (HROs), 59–60
   keys to, 61
   Kotagal, Dr. Uma, 58
   Krzyzewski, Mike, 51
   Mary Day Nursery, 50
   Mulligan, Terry, 52–55, *55*
   Solutions for Patient Safety
      (SPS), 58–60, *61*
   storytelling, 51–52
Coming Together Project,
      22, 25, 46
commitment, 69–76
   Considine, Gene and Howard,
      69–70, *70*
   families, 69–70
   Hirschbeck family, 70–74, *72*
   keys to, 76
   The Magic of Michael
      Foundation, 70–74, *72*
   Muransky, Ed, 71–73
   O'Desky, Patricia (Pat),
      73–75, *74*
communication, 62–68
   Father Norman Douglas,
      65–66, *66*
   Heart to Heart Communications,
      65–68, *67, 68*
   keys to, 68
   Knecht, Connie, 63–64, *65*
   Vuillemin, Larry, 65, *66*
community, 34–49
   Jackson, Dorothy O., 39–43, *40*

keys to, 49
Knepper, Dr. George, 47–49, *47*
Knight, John S. (Jack), 34–39, *36, 37*
Lieberth, David (Dave), 43–48, *44*
confidence, 77–83
   Burg, Eileen, 79–80, *79*
   Burg, Peter, 77–80, *79*
   Dambrot, Keith, 81–82, *82*
   I PROMISE School, 80–81, *81*
   James, David, 77–78, 81
   James, LeBron, 80–82
   keys to, 83
Considine, Cathryn (O'Malley), 1, 67, *68*
Considine, Gene and Howard, *iii*, 69–70, *70*
Considine, Rebecca (Becky), 1, 91, *94, 96, 126*
Considine, William (Bill), *96, 102, 108*, 125–127, *125, 126*
corporate citizenship, 98–116
   Akron Paint & Varnish, 109–110
   Babby, Ken/Akron Rubber-Ducks, 112–113, *113*
   GAR Foundation, 102–104, *103*
   Goodyear Tire & Rubber Company, 104–106
   keys to, 116
   LeafFilter, 110–112
   Marks Family/Blue Line, 100–102
   Ohio Edison/First Energy Corporation, 106–109
   Theken family of companies & NextStep Companies, 114–115
   Timken Foundation, 115–116

courage, 84–90
   children, 85
   Coles, Robert, 84
   Day, Dorothy, 84–85
   Judge Linda Teodosio, 85–90, *89*
   Judge William Kannel, 85–88
   keys to, 90
Court Appointed Special Advocate/Guardian Ad Litem (CASA/GAL), 87
culture, 12–18
   founding of Akron Children's Hospital, 15
   keys to, 18
   people, 15–16
   polio treatment, 14–15, *14*
   Sherman, Roger, 13–14, *13*, 16
   You Are This Hospital, 16–17

D
Dambrot, Keith, 81
David Lieberth Leadership Akron Award of Excellence, 46
Day, Dorothy, 84–85
Dennison, Jim, 95–97, *95, 96*
Douglas, Father Norman, 65–66, *66*
Downtown Akron Partnership, 46

E
Emerson, Ralph Waldo, 2–3

F
First Energy Corporation, 106–109
Fowler Family, *21*
Fowler, Reverend Dr. Ronald, 20–25, *21, 24*, 41
Frechette, Father Richard (Rick), 55–58, *56*
Friebert, Dr. Sarah, 26, 28–33, *29*

G

GAR Foundation, 102–104
Giermann, William (Bill), 48
Goman, Carol Kinsey, 50–51
Goodyear Foundation, 105
Goodyear Tire & Rubber Company, 104–106, *104*
Greater Akron Speaks Out for Values breakfast, *67–68*
Grigg, Richard (Dick), 60

H

H. Peter Burg Award, 9
Haslinger, Sandra, and Family, 32
health care, 121–122
Heart to Heart Communications, 65–68, *67, 68*
Heinz Poll Summer Dance Festival, 46
Hero Patients, 101, 108, *102*
Hero Zones, 101
high reliability organizations (HROs), 59–60
25 Hill, 108
Hirschbeck Family, *72*
Hirschbeck, Denise, 70–72, *72*
Hirschbeck, Erin, 70, *72*
Hirschbeck, John, 70–72, *72*
Hirschbeck, John Drew, 70–71
Hirschbeck, Megan, 70–71, *72*
Hirschbeck, Michael, 70–72
How to Boil Water and Other Things Too Good to Miss (Jackson), 42
Hoyt, Clark, 36, 38
HROs (high reliability organizations), 59–60

I

I PROMISE School, 46, 80–81, *81*
Ibarguen, Alberto, 35, 38–39
insurance, 121–122

J

Jackson, Cassidy, 30–32, *31*
Jackson, Dorothy O., 39–43, *40*
James, David, 77–78, 81
James, LeBron, 80–82
  I PROMISE School, 46, 80–81, *81*
John M. Eisenberg Patient Safety and Quality Award, 60, *61*
Jones Family, *108*
Jones, Charles E. (Chuck), 109, *108*
Joseph and Edna Josephson Institute of Ethics, 6

K

Kannel, Bea, 87
Kannel, Judge William, 85–88
Kapper, Ray, 94–95
Kaulig Giving, 112
Kaulig, Lisa, 110–112
Kaulig, Matt, 110–112, *111*
Kempf, Dr. Jeff, 57–58
Kempf, Dr. Ellen, 58
Knecht, Connie, 63–64, *65*
Knepper, Dr. George, 47–49, *47*
Knight Foundation, 35, 38–39
Knight Ridder Newspapers, 35
Knight, James L. (Jim), 34–35, 38–39, *36*
Knight, John S. (Jack), 34–39, *36, 37*
Kotagal, Dr. Uma, 58
Koufos, Kosta, *120*

Kramer, Richard J., 106
Krzyzewski, Mike, 51

L
Larson, Rev. Knute, 24–25, *24*
Lauer, Chuck S., 52–53, *53*
Leadership (Considine), 51, 53
Leadership Akron, 46, 48, 87
LeafFilter, 110–112
Lieberth, David (Dave), 43–48, *44*
Lives of Moral Leadership (Coles), 84
Loucks, Vern, 54–55
Love Akron Network, 21, 25, 43
Lucas (Rife), 117–118, *118, 119*

M
The Magic of Michael Foundation, 70–74, *72*
Main Street Gourmet, 100
Marks Family, 100–102, *100*
Marks, Jeannine, 100, *100*
Marks, Steve, 100–101, *100*
Mary Day Nursery, vi–viii, *vii, viii,* 15–16, 50
Matt and Lisa Kaulig Family Foundation, 112
Mayer, Christine Amer, 103
Maynard Family, *11*
Maynard Family Foundation, 5
Maynard, Philip H., 5–11, *11*
Maynard, Tomiko, 8, *11*
McKee, Robert, 51
Medicaid, 121
Modern Healthcare magazine, 52
Mulligan, Susan, 55
Mulligan, Terry, 52–55, *55*
Muransky, Ed, 71

N
NextStep Companies, 114–115
Njus, Dr. Glen O., 114

O
O'Desky, Patricia (Pat), 73–75, *74*
O'Malley, Cathryn (Considine), 1, 67, *68*
Ohio and Its People (Knepper), 49
Ohio Edison, 106–109
Orr, John, *108*

P
"Palette of Care" painting by Cassidy Jackson, 31–32, *31*
palliative care, 28–32
Parry, Stu, 95
Perkins, Colonel George Tod, vi–viii
Pfander, Jim, 113
Pike, Albert, 10
Plusquellic, Mayor Donald, 41
polio treatment, 14–15, *14*
Popik, Layla, 102

R
Rebecca D. Considine Research Institute, 123
Reddy Kilowatt, *106,* 107, *108*
Reed, Kathy, *94*
respect, 20
Rife Family, *118*
Rife, Amanda, *119*
Rife, Lucas, 117–118, *118, 119*
Roadway Express, Inc., 102
Roush, Galen, 102–103
Roush, Ruth, 103

S
Safe Mobility Project, 105
Santa PICsU, 112

Sawyer, Mayor Tom, 41
Schwartz Center Rounds, 33
SEI (Summit Education Initiative), 104
Sheridan, Bill, 2
Sherman, Roger, 13–14, 16, *13*
soap box derby, 107–108, *107*
Solutions for Patient Safety (SPS), 58–60, *61*
Spirit of Service newsletter, 16
SPS (Solutions for Patient Safety), 58–60, *61*
St. Damien Pediatric Hospital, 56–58
storytelling, 51–52
Summit Education Initiative (SEI), 104

T
teamwork. *See* collaboration
Teodosio, Andrea Rose, 88–89, *89*
Teodosio, Judge Linda, 85–90, *89*
Teodosio, Tom, 88–89
Theken, Randy, 114–115
This City Reads! literacy project, 22

Timken Foundation, 115–116, *116*
Timken, Henry H., Sr., 115
Torre, Joe, *72*
Tressel, Ellen, *96*
Tressel, Jim, 96–97, *96*
Trevor (Weigand), 119–120
Trevor Fund, 120

V
Venarge, Cheryl, 109
Venarge, Dave, 109–110, *110*
Venarge, Marcy, 109
Venarge, Tom, 109
Vuillemin, Larry, 65, *66*

W
Weigand Family, *120*
Weigand, Trevor, 119–120, *120*
William P. Kannel Juvenile Court Center, 86
Williams, Bernett, 23–24
Wingfoot One, *104*

Y
You Are This Hospital, 16–17